D0742177

Praise for *Active Value Investing*

"Reads like a conversation with Vitaliy: deep, insightful, inquisitive, and civilized."

—Nassim Nicholas Taleb, author of *The Black Swan*

More Praise for
The Little Book of Sideways Markets

"The Perma Bears, like Dr. Nouriel Roubini, are always looking down as they wait for the Apocalypse and a collapse in stock prices. The Perma Bulls, like most Wall Street strategists, are always looking up as they wait for the next New Paradigm and Long Boom. By contrast, Vitaliy Katsenelson lies on his side and sees a sideways market. With lively anecdotes and substantive evidence, Vitaliy teaches investors how to navigate and profit from a 'do nothing' market. Run, don't walk, to read Vitaliy's pearls of analytical wisdom!"

—Doug Kass, Seabreeze Partners Management Inc.

"Vitaliy Katsenelson has combined analytical rigor, market history, and common sense to produce a valuable, highly readable guide for investors seeking to navigate the investing environment of today and the years to come."

—Michael Santoli, columnist, *Barron's*

"And to think we thought sideways markets were impossible for investors. Vitaliy convinces us otherwise, with the most important lesson ever: Know when to sell!"

—Herb Greenberg, Senior Stocks Commentator, CNBC

"There is a lot of practical wisdom in this book for every investor. My personal favorite is 'Marry your stocks, but with a prenuptial agreement,' which is not only great advice but also sums up Vitaliy's own brand of intelligent investing. His is a style that has been informed not just by mathematical analysis, but also his practical experience—of which there are many useful examples—and especially his unique personal history, which informs every page. A worthwhile addition to every bookshelf, both physical and virtual!"

—Jeff Matthews Hedge Fund Manager and Author,
Pilgrimage to Warren Buffett's Omaha

"Expresses clearly the simple truths of successful investing today. Katsenelson has written the best book on understanding the dynamics of sideways or range-bound markets."

—Kim Shannon, CFA President and CIO, Sionna Investment Managers

"This book convincingly reinforces the timeless advice of contrarian value investing. Vitaliy Katsenelson concisely articulates how an investor may better weather the potentially difficult markets that lie ahead."

—Rob Arnott, Chairman, Founder, Research Affiliates

"The bad news is a go nowhere market. The good news is that this *Little Book* will show you in a big way how to take advantage to achieve market beating returns."

—Robert P. Miles, author, *The Warren Buffett CEO*

THE LITTLE BOOK

OF
SIDEWAYS
MARKETS

Little Book Big Profits Series

In the *Little Book Big Profits* series, the brightest icons in the financial world write on topics that range from tried-and-true investment strategies to tomorrow's new trends. Each book offers a unique perspective on investing, allowing the reader to pick and choose from the very best in investment advice today.

Books in the *Little Book Big Profits* series include:

THE LITTLE BOOK

OF
SIDEWAYS
MARKETS

How to Make Money in Markets
That Go Nowhere

VITALIY N. KATSENELSON

WILEY

John Wiley & Sons, Inc.

Published by John Wiley & Sons, Inc., Hoboken, New Jersey.
Published simultaneously in Canada.

For general information on our other products and services or for technical support, please contact our Customer Care Department within the United States at (800) 762-2974, outside the United States at (317) 572-3993 or fax (317) 572-4002.

Wiley also publishes its books in a variety of electronic formats. Some content that appears in print may not be available in electronic books. For more information about Wiley products, visit our web site at www.wiley.com.

Library of Congress Cataloging-in-Publication Data:

Katsenelson, Vitaliy N.
    The little book of sideways markets : how to make money in markets that go nowhere / Vitaliy Katsenelson.
        p.   cm. — (Little books. big profits ; 32)
    ISBN 978-0-470-93293-3 (cloth); ISBN 978-1-118-01035-8 (ebk);
    ISBN 978-1-118-01036-5 (ebk); ISBN 978-1-118-01037-2 (ebk)
        1. Stock exchanges.   2. Business cycles.   3. Investments.   I. Title.
    HG4551.K294   2010
    332.63'22—dc22
                                                                    2010042184

Printed in the United States of America

10 9 8 7 6 5 4 3 2 1

Contents

To
Jonah and Hannah

Foreword

≈

The End of the Debt Supercycle and Sideways Markets

It is common among market analysts to talk of <u>secular (long-term)</u> bull and bear markets, but back in the late 1990s I began to notice that markets didn't necessarily march to a neat and tidy bull or bear tune. In my book, _Bull's Eye Investing_, I explained that investors should focus on valuation instead of price, particularly when markets seem to tread water (lots of action, no prolonged movement up or down) for an extended period of time. In other words, there was a third type of secular market: the trendless market.

A few years later, Vitaliy Katsenelson came along and started talking about sideways (Cowardly Lion) markets.

What a clever way to describe these trendless, whipsaw markets that are terribly maddening to investors. This book is a helpful and easy-to-understand guide to navigating these frustrating periods. You need this guidance here and now, because markets are going to go nowhere for some time.

What is a secular sideways market and why do I say it will continue? To see tomorrow, let's take a look back in time. In doing so we'll be able to readily see how valuable this book will be for your portfolio.

A Little Perspective on Time and Behavior

Markets go from long periods of appreciation to long periods of stagnation. These cycles last on average 17 years. If you bought an index in the United States in 1966, it was 1982 before you saw a new high—that was the last secular sideways market in the United States (until the current one). Investing in that market was difficult, to say the least. But buying in the beginning of the next secular bull market in 1982 and holding until 1999 saw an almost 13 times return. Investing was simple and the rising markets made geniuses out of many investors and investment professionals. Since early 2000, markets in much of the developed world have basically been down to flat. Once again, we are in a difficult period. Genius is in short supply.

"But why?" I am often asked. Why don't markets just continue to go up as so many pundits say that "over the long term" they do? I agree that over the *very* long term, markets do go up. And therein is the problem: Most people are not in the market for *that* long—40 to 90 years. Maybe it's the human desire to live forever that has many focused on that super long-term market performance that looks so good. Or perhaps it is the habit people have of taking their most recent experience and projecting it into the future. As the previous century closed, a good many investors queried in surveys indicated that they thought they would make a compound 15 percent a year from their investments in the stock market. And that expectation was still there a few years later even after a brutal bear market. *Research shows that it takes at least three negative events to persuade people that things have changed.* This is usually just about the time that things are indeed getting ready to change for the better!

History, as Mark Twain said, does not repeat, but it does rhyme. In the 1930s and 1940s we had the Great Depression, a series of policy mistakes, and a war. Stock returns ended up in single digits as the second half of the century dawned. Then we had the boom of the 1950s and on into the 1960s, then a war, a series of policy mistakes, and the tumultuous 1970s with inflation and high interest rates. Then Paul Volcker wrenched the economy into two recessions, bringing stock market returns back to single digits (!). The next 18 years saw a perfect environment for a bull market: falling

interest rates and inflation, new technologies, and a demographic bulge designed to create bull markets and foster
optimism—even if punctuated by a recession and several
market crashes. As positive year after positive year passed,
many assumed that things would be even better the next year.
Trees really would grow to the sky.

Then came the bursting of the bubble and the Tech
Wreck, a recession, and a vicious short-term bear market in
stock prices, especially in the beloved tech sector. But things
soon got rolling again and the pundits were proclaiming
the return of the bull market. Artificially low rates from the
Federal Reserve, tax cuts, and what we now know was a bubble in housing jet-fueled an economic rise around the world.
Indeed, a study (co-authored by Alan Greenspan) showed
that better than 2 percent (and sometimes almost 3 percent!)
of gross domestic product (GDP) growth per year from 2002
to 2006 was basically from people taking out credit against
their houses. Without this line of credit, the recession would
have lasted over two full years and the next two would have
seen GDP growth in the range of a puny 1 percent.

And that brings us to the current environment.
Households in the United States and throughout the
developing world are beginning to cut back on debt, paying down old bills and taking out less in new debt. But
governments in many countries are borrowing ever more
money to fund their deficits.

The Endgame of the Debt Supercycle

If the mortgage meltdown was a wake-up call for overextended homeowners, Greece was a warning to governments everywhere that there is a limit to how much debt a government can carry before the lenders call in their IOUs or stop lending. Once the bond markets begin to think you either are not serious about controlling your debt or will not be able to pay it back at something approaching fair value, borrowing costs begin to rise, with interest taking an ever-larger portion of tax revenues. Today, Ireland's debt costs, even though the Irish are serious about cutting spending, are rising rapidly. Tomorrow? It will be any country that does not get its debt under control.

We may not have reached the bottom of the well, but we sense it is near. We have been in a debt supercycle—that ever-growing mountain of debt that has fueled growth—for 60 years. Trees don't grow to the sky and you can't keep piling up more and more debt that takes greater and greater chunks of your income (or GDP). A picture paints a thousand words: When you look at the chart on the next page that shows debt as a percentage of GDP, you clearly see how debt has grown at an ever-faster rate (in the United States, but the data points look very similar for many developed countries). Sometimes debt is good—when it is used for productive purposes such as building factories or creating

U.S. Debt as a % of GDP

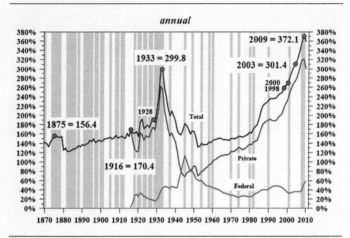

annual

Total

Private

Federal

2009 = 372.1

2003 = 301.4

2000
1998

1933 = 299.8

1928

1875 = 156.4

1916 = 170.4

Sources: Bureau of Economic Analysis, Federal Reserve, Census Bureau: Historical Statistics of the United States, Colonial Times to 1970. Through Q2 2010.

new businesses—but when it gets spent on consumption, it's just debt that doesn't pay its keep. Think of it this way: If you take out a loan to put your child through college, you are making an investment. When you put your dinner on a credit card and then take three months to pay it off, the debt returns nothing and actually causes your dinner to have cost more than the prices on the menu.

The stimulus bills of 2008 to 2009 helped feed this debt cycle. But even with the government spending, consumers and businesses seem to have wised up and are cutting their debt—even as the government is creating more!

Economics may not be a hard-and-fast science like physics but it does contain at least one mathematical equation that holds true for all countries at all times:

$$GDP = C + I + G + (E - i)$$

or, GDP is equal to Consumption (Consumer and Business) + Investment + Government Spending + Net Exports (Exports − Imports).

The Keynesian economic school of thought says that when C (consumption) is weak, the government should run deficits to boost demand until the consumer is back and ready to spend. This will work. The last stimulus bill that went through the United States and much of Europe had a positive effect on final demand and GDP. But it did so by adding trillions to the debt side of the equation.

We are coming to the limits of government's ability to borrow. In some countries, that limit is very close, whereas in others like the United States, it is a few years off; but people everywhere are waking up to the fact that fiscal deficits need to be brought under control so that their country will not end up with the disastrous choices that Greece and some other countries now face. Don't even get me started on Japan. Japan is a bug in search of a windshield. I leave it to Vitaliy to explain that problem, as you'll read in Chapter 15.

Here is where the equation shows another reality. Reducing any input to the equation is a drag on total GDP. Therefore, if G (government spending) is reduced it will be a drag on GDP. Normally, balanced budgets can be brought about by controlling spending and letting normal growth of an economy catch up with the deficits. But country after country has let their fiscal deficits rise so much, and growth is so weak, that it is going to take either serious spending cuts or new taxes to help bring about the reduction of the fiscal deficits.

In their brilliant and wide-sweeping book, *This Time Is Different* (Princeton University Press, 2009), Professors Carmen Reinhart and Kenneth Rogoff studied 250 financial crises in 60 countries over the past few hundred years. One of their findings is that in the aftermath of credit-crisis-induced recessions, it takes at least six to eight years for countries to get back to normal growth. The ensuing years from the onset of crisis are characterized by slow growth and more volatile and frequent recessions. This follows from countries and their citizens having to get their balance sheets in order, and the former credit induced growth having to now come from a more natural state of organic economic growth, fueled mostly by rising productivity. Slower growth means less of a cushion for normal economic ebbs and flows that seem to occur, like the weather (economic crises will happen from time to time, not unlike stormy weather). In 1998, the U.S. economy was very strong and could weather an Asian crisis, even as the economy slowed somewhat. Today? The same event would likely push us into a recession.

To the extent that a country can encourage private businesses to invest and start up and current businesses to find new markets and adapt, the length of recessions and slower-growth periods are reduced. The data from Reinhart and Rogoff show that government spending on stimulus, while providing the illusion of the government doing something and a short-term boost (like steroids), does not add to real GDP. Real growth must come from the private sector.

And that takes time. It is just the way it is. Starting a new business that succeeds is not short work. The majority of new businesses fail within five years. But the research shows that new private businesses are the group that creates the net new jobs. Not big business or even small business, but start-ups!

Which Brings Us Back to the Beginning

With the reduction in government spending being a long-term good but a short-term drag, it takes time for a country to get back to a sustainable national budget, because it takes time for a new and thriving private sector to emerge and have the wherewithal to pay more taxes. And that means we will be in a slower-growth muddle–through economy with uncomfortably higher unemployment for the better part of this next decade. And that means a slower-growth environment for equities from developed countries, which means that you need a new perspective to successfully navigate today's equity markets. You need a different strategy, and Vitaliy helps you find it.

Let's rewind to two points: (1) The data are clear that in the years following a credit crisis, recessions are more volatile and frequent than usual. (2) It typically takes at least three negative events to convince investors that something different is indeed happening. And that is what we are likely to get in the coming six to seven years, which just happens to be the years remaining on the average secular sideways market cycle clock.

Hmmmm.

Could it be that we will see, as we have in past cycles, that stock market valuations in the United States and the rest of the developed world keep dropping? Will they make the full trip as they have done in the past? And will those low valuations, coupled with countries finally (!) getting their fiscal houses in order (and thus removing the drag of a slowing "G") and the entry of a whole slew of new technologies developing in the interim, act like a tightly coiled spring, launching yet another secular bull market cycle? Wouldn't that be an interesting rhyme?

Another thought: There are any number of emerging market countries that are just at the beginning of their debt supercycle. They are not hampered by too much debt, because (luckily for them!) nobody would lend to them. They have a newfound zeal for markets and entrepreneurship. Pay some attention, as they will soon chart their own course apart from the developed world.

In the meantime, we are in a market environment where investors have to be more actively engaged in their investments than before during a bull market when the rising tide lifted all ships. *The Little Book of Sideways Markets* is a life preserver that will help you navigate these perilous waters. Wear it well and wisely.

—John Mauldin

John Mauldin is president of Millennium Wave Investments, three-time best-selling New York Times author, and author of the upcoming The Endgame, The End of the Debt Supercycle *(John Wiley & Sons). He is also the writer of the free weekly e-letter,* Thoughts from the Frontline, *which goes to more than 1.5 million people. For more information, please visit www.johnmauldin.com.*

Acknowledgments

First and foremost, I want to express my deepest gratitude to my parents, for believing in me. They always saw a greater potential in me than I believed I possessed, at every step along the way. Through their guidance and never-ending encouragement I rose to be what *they* saw in me, not to what *I* thought I could achieve. Nobody has been more surprised at my achievements than I have. I'll try to do the same for my kids.

I would like to thank: Michael Conn—my sounding board, my friend, my partner at Investment Management Associates (IMA); Barry Pasikov—I am sure our daily phone conversations spilled onto the pages of this book; Aleksandr Sheykhet—I neglected to express my extreme gratitude for his help with my first book; E. Jake Berzon, my consigliore, for putting a magnifying glass to every page; Charley Sweet, for helping make these pages shine; Michael Mauboussin for his hold-no-prisoners, constructive feedback; Jeffrey Scharf, Ed Durica, Hewitt Heiserman, and Kane Cotton for their terrific feedback; my brother Alex Katsenelson, for drawing a picture of Golde and her offsprings as Tevye would have drawn them, in the valuation chapter; my terrific editors at John Wiley & Sons, Pamela van Giessen and Emilie Herman; my wife Rachel, for taking care of the Katsenelson household, which includes two wonderful but time-consuming children, Jonah and Hannah, while I was locked up in the basement writing this and my earlier book; and to my aunt Anna Lerer for bringing my family from Russia to the United States. I often pinch myself and constantly remind my kids of how lucky we are to live in this wonderful country.

—Vitaliy N. Katsenelson

Introduction

MY FATHER'S YOUNGER SISTER LEFT MOSCOW in 1979. I'm not sure whether she was the first Jewish/Russian immigrant to discover Brighton Beach, but she definitely found it before Russian became its primary language. In 1991 she invited my family to the United States. By that time my aunt had divorced and re-married. Her new husband was a rabbi who led a congregation in Cheyenne, Wyoming. With apologies to Wyoming, thankfully we did not move to Cheyenne, but settled about 100 miles south—in Denver.

After folding towels at the health club, busing tables at the Village Inn, and bagging groceries, my first real job was at an investment firm in Golden, Colorado.

I was a junior at the University of Colorado. I was hired because of my computer skills. I wrote a database application that they still use today. They didn't have anything else for me to do computer-wise, so I was promoted to head trader. (Okay, I was their only trader.) *Trader* was a glorified term for my actual position since all I really did was call or fax buy and sell orders. But the job gave me an opportunity to spend a lot of time in front of a Bloomberg terminal and allowed me to talk stocks with portfolio managers. It did not take me long to realize that I loved investing. I changed my major for the sixth and final time, and the rest was history . . . well, almost.

I wanted to be an analyst and they did not need one, so I pulled out the Yellow Pages and sent my résumé to every single investment firm in Denver. I don't know what Michael Conn, Investment Management Associates, Inc. (IMA)'s president, saw in me, since I didn't know much then—perhaps my ambition and hunger for knowledge stood out. Finding somebody willing to pay me to analyze stocks was almost unbelievable.

IMA had been around since 1979 and had a solid investment record. Since its founding, it had owned high-quality companies that consistently grew earnings and traded at reasonable valuations. On my very first day at work Michael Conn, now my partner, proudly showed me his positions in Walgreens, MBNA, and a few other stocks that he had bought more than a decade earlier. His cost basis was a fraction of their current prices, and many stocks were up 10- and 20-fold since he bought them. Buy and hold worked!

The years 1997 and 1998 were great for IMA; its stocks went up as much as the market, which was plenty—the market was up around 30 percent each year. But 1999 was a different story. The "reasonable" valuation requirement kept the firm away from the dot-coms and the majority of high-tech companies, as their business models made no sense. In 1999 the bubbly stocks were doubling every other month, while our stodgy, high-quality companies lagged. The Standard & Poor's (S&P) 500 index was up over 20 percent in 1999, and our stocks were barely up. Our clients were grouchy, but our past success sustained their goodwill. The next year our patience was rewarded—our stocks went up, while the market, especially the dot-coms, and tech crashed. We felt vindicated, but vindication was short-lived.

That was the last year when the time-honored strategy of buying and holding great companies at reasonable valuations worked. In the next few years the market either declined or stagnated. We were stagnating, too. We had a few years of frustration to ride out. At first, I thought it was a 1999-like phenomenon: Our stocks were temporarily out of favor; but after all, we owned great companies, so how could we go wrong?

The "Aha!" moment came when a speaker at an investment conference I attended put up a Dow Jones chart in logarithmic scale (similar to the one in Chapter 1) and pointed out that every time the Dow got to a handle of 1 with zeros behind it (e.g., 100, 1000) it stagnated for more than a decade. This was early 2004, and Dow was bouncing around 10,000, so the speaker thought it was an appropriate time for the market to stagnate. He did not explain as to why this should happen—and I was not impressed with his "every time we hit 1 with zeros" logic. Still, he got me thinking about whether there might be a rational explanation to the pattern he described.

I began a quest to find out. I pored over a century of stock market and economic data, and discovered that there was indeed a very logical explanation as to why there are times when the market goes nowhere for decades. You'll have to read this book to find out what I learned, but I'll tell you this much right off the top: It has very little to do with a 1 with zeros attached to it.

The same way that most people are born into their religion, as an investor I was born into my investment strategy, the IMA strategy, the day I came to work for the firm. I was weaned on owning high-quality companies that grow earnings and traded at reasonable valuations, naturally I believed that our investment strategy was superior to all others. However, a few years of failure and frustration are a good catalyst for reassessing one's belief system. After careful examination I found some major flaws with our strategy.

Our stocks were reasonably priced—we expected to make money on them, because their earnings would rise over time and that would pull the stock prices up. But they were not cheap, thus they could not afford to disappoint Wall Street. If the company's earnings came out just a few pennies short, the stock was taken out back and shot. These flaws were varnished over by the bull market of the 1980s and 1990s, when all stocks rose; but a stagnating market is like a giant magnifying glass that shows all flaws in high relief. The valuations of our stocks were reasonable only if the overall valuations of the past bull market were to persist into the future, but my research led me to believe that this would not happen for a long, long time. We had bought and rarely sold; in fact, we prided ourselves on having low turnover in our portfolios. The painful realization we came to was that buy and hold was not really dead but in a long-term coma, awaiting the next secular bull market, which was far, far away.

We had to change the way we invested.

I took our existing process, modified it for sideways markets, added tools and a framework I developed, and supersized it with a margin of safety. We did not want to own stocks that were reasonably priced; we wanted them to be unreasonably cheap. Value investment principles were at the core of our strategy, so there was no reason to reinvent the wheel, but we put away our buy-and-hold shingle to become buy-and-sell investors. Michael Conn, who is 30 years my senior and had been investing for over three decades, was willing to change how we invested when presented with new evidence—I deeply respect and admire that. This is the story of how we became active value investors.

The new investment process spilled into a book that I started writing in 2005 and that was published in 2007 by John Wiley & Sons: *Active Value Investing: Making Money in Range-Bound Markets*. Since it came out, I've given dozens of speeches around the world, participated in many debates, and given hundreds of interviews. It is probably fair to say that I've now given the subject of sideways markets even more thought than I had prior to the publishing of my first book. I've figured out how to explain the process better, and I've learned a few new things. Also, over the past three years, the global economy has changed and our investment strategy must be adapted to the very different economic reality into which we're being propelled. It seemed time to distill the essence of my latest research and analysis into this *Little Book*, which, unlike my first book, is written not just for my peers (investment professionals and serious, I-cannot-live-without-the-stock-market investors), but for sophisticated, curious readers who are interested in the stock market, but who are not pros.

Since this is a *Little Book*, I'll spare you the pain of wading through dozens of boring statistical tables and charts; however, if you get a sudden, uncontrollable urge to see them, you can either find them in *Active Value Investing* or access them (completely free) at ActiveValueInvesting.com.

Chapter One

Fasten Your Seat Belt

———— ❧ ————

Sideways Markets Are Here to Stay

GET READY FOR A GREAT ROLLER-COASTER RIDE in the markets. For the next decade or so the Dow Jones Industrial Average and the S&P 500 index will likely do what they did over the preceding decade: go up and down, setting all-time highs and multiyear lows along the way. But at the end of the ride, index and buy-and-hold stock investors, having experienced ups and downs and swings akin to those on an amusement park ride, will find themselves pretty much back where they started. This is all well and fine for visitors to Six Flags, but not really what most of us want for our investments and savings.

The length, the velocity, and the twists of the ride are yet to be written by history, but the flat long-term trajectory has been ordained by the 18-year bull market that ended in 2000. Using history as a guide, until about 2020 (give or take a few years) the U.S. stock market will likely continue to stagnate. Welcome to the sideways market!

Take a Trip to the Zoo

When we think of market direction we think in binary terms: bull—going up, and bear—declining. But what about markets that go nowhere over time? They are known as sideways markets and they look quite different from bear markets, although the distinction is seldom made. *All* long-term markets of the last century, with one exception, were either bull or sideways.* Since investors are used to associating animals with the direction of the market, I suggest a moniker for the sideways market:

---

*A few weeks after my first book *Active Value Investing: Making Money in Range-Bound Markets* came out, I started to regret calling the market range-bound, as I constantly was asked, "What is the range?" In the book, I never suggested I knew the range of these markets, but the book's name suggested otherwise. "Sideways" is a more accurate and less technical description of these very real markets, and it is the term I adapted for use in the present book.

the cowardly lion, whose bursts of occasional bravery lead to stock appreciation but are ultimately overrun by fear that leads to a descent.

We also split trends by how long they last. A *secular* market describes a state that lasts more than five years, perhaps taking place only once in a generation. A *cyclical* state is a significantly shorter market cycle that lasts a few months to a few years. When I discuss *secular* bull, bear, or sideways markets, I'll refer to them just as bull, bear, and sideways markets. I'll use the word *cyclical* when referencing cyclical markets.

During the twentieth century, almost every protracted bull market lasted about a decade and a half or so and was followed by a cowardly lion market that lasted just as long. For evidence, see Exhibit 1.1. The only exception was the Great Depression, where the bull market was followed by a bear market. Sideways and bear markets are radically different in nature and your investment strategies need to be radically different, too.

Let's look at a really long-term picture of the market. In Exhibit 1.1, we see that our current sideways market started on the heels of the 1982–2000 secular bull market. Since then, as you see in Exhibit 1.2, we have had a two-and-a-half-year cyclical (short-term) bear market, followed by a four-year cyclical bull market and then an all too familiar 50 percent decline that has been followed by

Exhibit 1.1   Bull or Sideways, Dow Jones Industrial Average, 100 Years and Counting

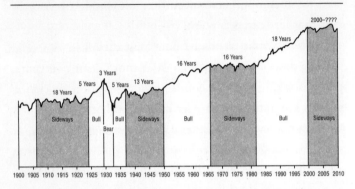

Exhibit 1.2   2000–2010 Dow Jones Industrial Average Sideways Foxtrot

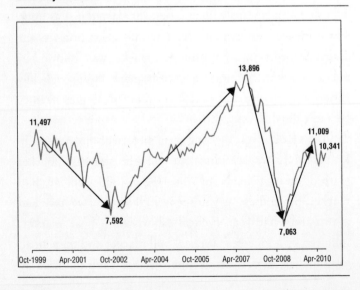

a nice bounce since March 2009. Altogether, the market hasn't gone anywhere in more than 10 years. If you are a long-term investor in an index fund or buying and holding, you are pretty much where you started 10 years ago.

It Takes (At Least) Two

Ask an investor what the stock market will do over the next decade and he'll tell you his expectations for the economy and earnings growth and then turn them into a projection for the market. This kind of thinking only looks at half of the equation that explains stock market (and individual stock) returns, while ignoring a very important variable that is responsible for a significant part of stock returns: the price-to-earnings (P/E) ratio. The P/E tells us what investors are paying for a dollar of earnings: A $15 stock of a company that earned $1 last year is trading at a P/E of 15.

Stock prices in the long run (not minutes or days, but years) are driven by two factors: earnings growth and changes in valuation (P/E ratio). Add a return from dividends, and you've captured all the variables responsible for the *total* return from stocks. The following equation*

---

*This equation is imprecise because it ignores the power of compounding. For clarity I am using simple addition and subtraction, as opposed to doing the precise thing by multiplying and dividing. In future chapters, to simplify the illustration of concepts, I'll continue to be imprecise with my formulas for the sake of clarity, by ignoring compounding.

(don't worry, this is the only one in the entire book) illus-
trates this:

$$\text{Stock's total return} = \text{Earnings growth/decline} \\ + \text{change in P/E} \\ + \text{dividend yield}$$

I hate the use of formulas in investing, as they usually
do more harm than good (especially the ones with fancy
Greek symbols), but this one is actually helpful and not
dangerous.

I dug up economic and stock market data for the last
100 years, sliced it and diced it in different ways, and
came to only one possible conclusion: Performance of the
economy and earnings growth did not vary much between
cowardly lion and bull markets. Although in the short run
the rates of economic and earnings growth were responsible for (cyclical) swings in the market, in the longer run,
as long as we had an average economy (not super-good or
super-bad), the animal in charge of the market was either
the bull or the cowardly lion.

Feeling Skeptical? It's Okay

If someone else was making a prediction that markets will
be sideways for another decade and he was relying on
past data to make this disturbing claim, I'd be skeptical.

After all, the past has passed and the future may be different. If you are feeling a bit wary about what I've said so far, you have a right to be, but hang on as I present the case. As you'll see, this prediction is less wacky than it appears at first.

I am an investor. I live and breathe stocks and have little patience for theoretical discussions. Thus, this is not a theoretical little tome. It is a practical guide to value investing in sideways markets. In Chapters 2 and 3 I explain what sideways markets are and how they will impact us. Then I put you in the shoes of a value investor through the story of Tevye—the milkman, farmer, and value investor. Finally, I introduce you to the framework for guiding your stock analysis that takes into account the lingering effects of the Great Recession, the financial crisis of 2008–2009, and the coming impact of the economic conditions in Japan and China so that you will be able to steer your portfolio safely and steadily in the face of continued uncertainties.

Chapter Two

A Sideways View
of the World

*What Happens in a
Sideways Market*

MOST PEOPLE (MYSELF INCLUDED) find discussions about stock markets a bit esoteric; for us, it is a lot easier to relate to individual stocks. Since a stock market is just a collection of individual stocks, let's take a look at a very typical sideways stock first: Wal-Mart. It will give us insight into what takes place in a sideways market (see Exhibit 2.1).

Exhibit 2.1   Wal-Mart Typical Sideways Market Stock

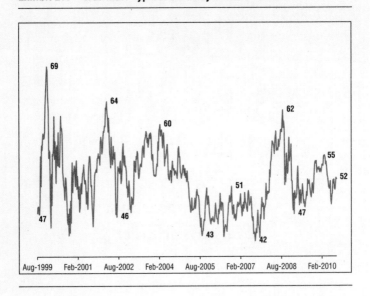

Though its shareholders experienced plenty of volatility over the past 10 years, the stock has gone nowhere—it fell prey to a cowardly lion.

Over the last decade Wal-Mart's earnings almost tripled from $1.25 per share to $3.42, growing at an impressive rate of 11.8 percent a year. This doesn't look like a stagnant, failing company; in fact, it's quite an impressive performance for a company whose sales are approaching half a trillion dollars. However, its stock chart led you to believe otherwise. The culprit responsible for this unexciting performance was valuation—the P/E—which declined from 45 to 13.7, or about 12.4 percent a year. The stock has not gone anywhere, as all the benefits from earnings growth were canceled out by a declining P/E. Even though revenues more than doubled and earnings almost tripled, all of the return for shareholders of this terrific company came from dividends, which did not amount to much.

This is exactly what we see in the broader stock market, which is comprised of a large number of companies whose stock prices have gone and will go nowhere in a sideways market.

Let's zero in on the last sideways market the United States saw, from 1966 to 1982. Earnings grew about 6.6 percent a year, while P/Es declined 4.2 percent; thus stock prices went up roughly 2.2 percent a year. As you can see in Exhibit 2.2, a secular sideways market is full of little (cyclical) bull and bear markets. The 1966–1982 market had five cyclical bull and five cyclical bear markets.

This is what happens in sideways markets: Two forces work against each other. The benefits of earnings growth are wiped out by P/E compression (the staple of sideways markets); stocks don't go anywhere for a long time, with plenty of (cyclical) volatility, while you patiently collect your dividends, which are meager in today's environment.

Exhibit 2.2   Don't Let Your Emotions Make You Miss These Cyclical Bulls and Bears (Dow Jones Industrial Average 1966–1982)

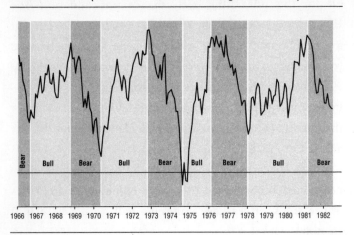

A quick glimpse at the current sideways market shows a similar picture: P/Es declined from 30 to 19, a rate of 4.6 percent a year, while earnings grew 2.4 percent. This explains why we are now pretty much where we were in 2000.

Bulls, Bears, and Cowardly Lions—Oh My

Exhibit 2.3 describes economic conditions and starting P/Es required for each market cycle. Historically, earnings growth, though it fluctuated in the short term, was very similar to the growth of the economy (GDP), averaging about 5 percent a year. If the market's P/E did not change

Exhibit 2.3   Economic Growth + Starting P/E = ?

Market	Economic Growth	Starting Valuation (P/E)
Bull	Average	Low
Sideways	Average	High
Bear	Bad	High

and *always* remained at its average of 15, then we would not have bull or sideways market cycles—we'd have no secular market cycles, period! Stock prices would go up with earnings growth, which would fluctuate due to normal economic cyclicality but would average about 5 percent, and investors would collect an additional approximately 4 percent in dividends. That is what would happen in a utopian world where people are completely rational and unemotional. But as Yoda might have put it, the utopian world is not, and people rational are not.

The P/E's journey from one extreme to the other is completely responsible for sideways and bull markets: P/E's ascent from low to high caused bull markets, and P/E's descent from high to low was responsible for the roller-coaster ride of sideways markets.

Bear markets happened when you had two conditions in place, a high starting P/E and prolonged economic distress; together they are a lethal combination. High P/Es reflect high investor expectations for the economy. Economic blues such as runaway inflation, severe deflation, declining or stagnating earnings, or a combination of these things sour these high expectations. Instead of an above-average economy, investors wake up to an economy that is below average. Presto, a bear market has started.

Let's examine the only secular bear market in the twentieth century in the United States: the period of the Great Depression. P/Es declined from 19 to 9, at a rate of about 12.5 percent a year, and earnings growth was not there to soften the blow, since earnings declined 28.1 percent a year. Thus stock prices declined by 37.5 percent a year!

Ironically—and this really tells you how subjective is this whole "science" that we call investing—the stock market decline from 1929 to 1932 doesn't fit into a "secular" definition, since it lasted less than five years. Traditional, by-the-book, secular markets should last longer than five years. I still put the Great Depression into the secular category, as it changed investor psyches for generations. Also, it was a very significant event: Stocks declined almost 90 percent, and 80 years later we are still talking about it.*

---

*What if we start with low valuations and contracting earnings (i.e., a bad economy)? Though this has not happened for over 100 years, the combination would likely lead to either a mild bear market or a sideways market. The outcome would depend on how low the starting P/E was and how bad was the economic decline.

However, a true, by the book, long-term bear market took place in Japan. Starting in the late 1980s, over a 14-year period, Japanese stocks declined 8.2 percent a year. This decline was driven by a complete collapse of both earnings—which declined 5.3 percent a year—and P/Es, which declined 3 percent a year. Japanese stocks were in a bear market because stocks were expensive, and earnings declined over a long period of time. In bear markets *both* P/Es and earnings decline.

In sideways markets P/E ratios decline. They say that payback is a bitch, and that is what sideways markets are all about: Investors pay back in declining P/Es for the excess returns of the preceding bull market.

Let's move to a slightly cheerier subject: the bull market. We see a great example of a secular bull market in the 1982–2000 period. Earnings grew about 6.5 percent a year and P/Es rose from very low levels of around 10 to the unprecedented level of 30, adding another 7.7 percent to earnings growth. Add up the positive numbers and you get super-juicy compounded stock returns of 14.7 percent a year. Sprinkle dividends on top and you have incredible returns of 18.2 percent over almost two decades. No surprise that the stock market became everyone's favorite pastime in the late 1990s.

The Price of Humanity

Is 100 years of data enough to arrive at any kind of meaningful conclusion about the nature of markets? Academics would argue that we'd need thousands of years' worth of stock market data to come to a statistically significant conclusion. They would be right, but we don't have that luxury. I am not making an argument that sideways markets follow bull markets based on statistical significance; I simply don't have enough data for that.

Most of the time common stocks are subject to irrational and excessive price fluctuations in both directions as the consequence of the ingrained tendency of most people to speculate or gamble . . . to give way to hope, fear and greed.

—*Benjamin Graham*

As the saying goes, the more things change the more they remain the same. Whether a trade is submitted by telegram, as was done at the turn of the twentieth century, or through the screen of an online broker, as is the case today, it still has a human originating it. And all humans come with standard emotional equipment that is, to some degree, predictable. Over the years we've become more educated, with access to fancier, faster, and better financial tools. A myriad of information is accessible at our fingertips, with speed and abundance that just a decade ago was available to only a privileged few.

Despite all that, we are no less human than we were 10, 50, or 100 years ago. We behave like humans, no matter how sophisticated we become. Unless we completely delegate all our investment decision making to computers, markets will still be impacted by human emotions.

The following example highlights the psychology of bull and cowardly lion markets:

During a bull market stock prices go up because earnings grow and P/Es rise. So in the absence of P/E change, stocks would go up by, let's say, 5 percent a year due to earnings growth. But remember, in the beginning stages of a bull market P/Es are depressed, thus the first phase of P/E increase is normalization, a journey towards the mean; and as P/Es rise they juice up stock returns by, we'll say, 7 percent a year. So stocks prices go up 12 percent (5 percent due to earnings growth and 7 percent due to P/E increase), and that is without counting returns from dividends. After a while investors become accustomed to their stocks rising 12 percent a year. At some point, though, the P/E crosses the mean mark, and the second phase kicks in: The P/E heads towards the stars. A new paradigm is born: 12 percent price appreciation is the "new average" and the phrase *this time is different* is heard across the land.

Fifty or 100 years ago, "new average" returns were justified by the advancements of railroads, electricity, telephones, or efficient manufacturing. Investors mistakenly attributed high stock market returns that came from expanding P/Es to the economy, which despite all the advancements did not turn into a super-fast grower.

In the late 1990s, during the later stages of the 1982–2000 bull market, similar observations were made, except the names of the game changers were now just-in-time inventory, telecommunications, and the Internet. However, it is rarely different, and *never* different when P/E increase is the single source of the supersized returns. P/Es rose and went through the average (of 15) and far beyond. Everybody had to own stocks. Expectations were that the "new average" would persist —12 percent a year became your birthright rate of return.

P/Es can shoot for the stars, but they never reach them. In the late stage of a secular bull market P/Es stop rising. Investors receive "only" a return of 5 percent from earnings growth—and they are disappointed. The love affair with stocks is not over, but they start diversifying into other asset classes that recently provided better returns (real estate, bonds, commodities, gold, etc.).

Suddenly, stocks are not rising 12 percent a year, not even 5 percent, but closer to zero—P/E decline is wiping out any benefits from earnings growth of 5 percent and the "lost decade" (or two) of a sideways market has begun.

This Time Is *Not* Different

I've done a few dozen presentations on the sideways markets since 2007. I've found that people are either very happy or extremely *un*happy with this sideways market argument. The different emotional responses had nothing to do with how I dressed, but they correlated with the stock-market cycle we were in at the time of the presentation.

In 2007, when everyone thought we were in a new leg of the 1982 bull market, I was glad that eggs were not served while I presented my sideways thesis, for surely they would have been thrown at me. In late 2008 and early 2009, my sideways market message was a ray of sunlight in comparison to the Great Depression II mood of the audience.

Every cyclical bull market is perceived as the beginning of the next secular bull market, while every cyclical bear market is met with fear that the next Great Depression is upon us. Over time stocks become incredibly cheap again and their dividend yields finally become attractive. The sideways market ends, and a bull market ensues.

Where You Stand Will Determine How Long You Stand

The stock market seems to suffer from some sort of multiple personality disorder. One personality is in a chronic state of extreme happiness, and the other suffers from severe depression. Rarely do the two come to the surface at once. Usually one dominates the other for long periods of time. Over time, these personalities cancel each other out, so on average the stock market is a rational fellow. But rarely does the stock market behave in an average manner.

Among the most important concepts in investing is mean reversion, and unfortunately it is often misunderstood. The mean is the average of a series of low and high numbers—fairly simple stuff. The confusion arises in the application of reversion to the mean concept. Investors often assume that when mean reversion takes place the figures in question settle at the mean, but it just ain't so.

Although P/Es may settle at the mean, that is not what the concept of mean reversion implies; rather, it suggests *tendency* (direction) of a movement towards the mean. Add human emotion into the mix and P/Es turn into a pendulum—swinging from one extreme to the other (just as investors' emotions do) while spending very little time in the center. Thus, it is rational to expect that a period of above-average P/Es should be followed by a period of below-average P/Es and vice versa.

Since 1900, the S&P 500 traded on average at about 15 times earnings. But it spent only a quarter of the time between P/Es of 13 and 17—the "mean zone," two points above and below average. In the majority of cases the market reached its fair valuation only in passing from one irrational extreme to the other.

Mean reversion is the Rodney Dangerfield of investing: It gets no respect. Mean reversion is as important to investing as the law of gravity is to physics. As long as humans come equipped with the standard emotional equipment package, market cycles will persist and the pendulum will continue to swing from one extreme to the other.

Chapter Three

Don't Shoot the Messenger

How the Story Ends

O<small>NE HAS TO BE VERY CAREFUL WITH</small> the "E" in the P/E equation. There are usually no qualms about the "P"—it is what it is. The S&P 500 is trading at 1,122.8 as I am typing this in August 2010; that is the "P." But the "E" is a whole different animal.

"E" often requires *normalization,* as earnings are impacted tremendously by where we are in the economic cycle at a given time. Blindly using "E" without normalization will lead you to the wrong conclusions when you analyze the stock market and individual stocks. In Exhibit 3.1, P/Es for past market cycles are computed based on 12-month trailing earnings; however, I used 2010 estimated earnings to demonstrate current market valuation. Here is the rub: Estimates for 2010 reported and operating earnings for the S&P 500 are $75 and $45, respectively. A significant difference between two numbers is the "one-time" charges that never end up being one-time. I arrived at my "E" of $60 by averaging these two numbers.

Exhibit 3.1   Starting and Ending P/Es Based on 1-Year Trailing (Reported) Earnings of S&P 500

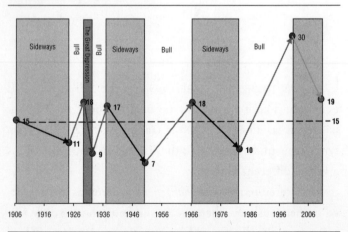

However, a better way to deal with the volatility of "E" in the P/E equation, when we attempt to value the market is to use 10-year trailing earnings. We use the current "P" but then average earnings over the preceding 10-year period. Don't worry, I won't ask you to compute the average (free computation is included in the steep price of this book; see Exhibit 3.2).

I'll admit, since investors never look at P/Es of individual stocks computed on 10-year trailing earnings, they are not very intuitive. However, when we look at the stock

Exhibit 3.2   Starting and Ending P/Es Based on 10-Year Trailing (Reported) Earnings of S&P 500

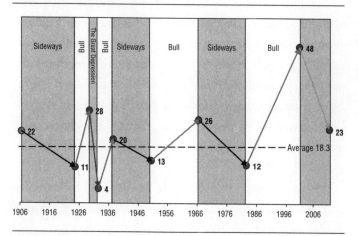

market, 10-year trailing P/Es' tendency to smooth out (normalize) the impact of economic cyclicality on earnings is very useful.

When will the current sideways market end and at what P/E? In Exhibits 3.1 and 3.2, I have computed starting and ending P/Es for every market cycle during the past century. As you can see, both exhibits tell the same story: The current sideways market started at the highest P/E level of any bull market we've seen in the United States.

The higher the valuations of stocks at the beginning of a sideways market, the longer that market is likely to last. It takes more time, and plenty of volatility, to deflate a higher starting P/E to a below-average one.

It is also apparent from these exhibits that even after investors received close to 10 years of little or no returns from the broad market indexes, S&P 500 P/E ratios were still close to the levels where previous sideways markets only started. The stock market is not cheap! Even though sideways markets in the twentieth century lasted from 13 to 18 years, the current sideways market has all the makings in place to become the longest in modern history.

Stocks are unlikely to settle at their fair valuation—they never did, at least in the twentieth century. This time is not likely to be different.

To paraphrase Mark Twain: History doesn't repeat itself, but it often rhymes. One outcome appears to be likely: The market will bottom at a rhyming 12 months trailing P/E that will fall significantly below the historical average of 15 just as it did at the end of each sideways market in the twentieth century.

Where Are We?

By mid-2010, 10 years after the 1982–2000 bull market concluded, a year after the Great Recession of 2008–2009 ended, valuations are still high, as stocks are trading at more than 19 times 2010 earnings. Both Exhibits 3.1 and 3.2 show that today's market valuation is at an above-average level, and that we are far away from the ending, below-average P/E; and so the sideways market marches on.

Setting Earnings Growth on Cruise Control

Imagine a train leaving High-P/E Station, cruising towards Low-P/E Station at a certain rate. The duration of this journey is set by distance and speed. The higher the starting P/E or the lower the ending one is, the longer the journey between them. The higher the speed—the rate of nominal (including inflation) earnings growth—the less time it will take to get from High-P/E Station to Low-P/E Station.

The rate of earnings growth—the speed of the train—is not constant. It fluctuates significantly in the short run, accelerating and decelerating with economic cyclicality; but despite annual fluctuations, from 1930 to 2000 long-term average nominal earnings growth varied only a few percentage points from the average and was about 5 percent (inflation was about 3 percent).

Now that we have this little framework, the question of how long becomes a seventh-grade algebra problem. I'll use the 10-year trailing earnings numbers to demonstrate it. The train left the high P/E station at 23 times earnings (current valuation) and will reach its final destination—the low P/E station—at 13 times earnings (past valuations were in that range). The train will be traveling at an average speed of 5 percent a year—our nominal earnings growth. How many years will it take for the train to reach its destination? The answer is 11.7 years.

The growth rate and final P/E are the wild cards that will decide how long the sideways markets will last. Nominal growth has two components that we would have to estimate to come up with the number: real earnings growth and inflation or deflation. As a consequence of the Great Recession, we'll likely face higher interest rates and higher taxes and thus lower economic growth. So, if real economic growth will be 1 percent lower than in the past, and assuming that inflation remains the same and average earnings growth is 4 instead of 5 percent, then it will take about 14.5 years for the sideways market to end.

There is nothing precise about estimating the length of the sideways market; I am just using the math to illustrate the relationships between different variables.

Are we going to have inflation or deflation in the future? I simply don't know. Inflation appears to be a higher-probability scenario than deflation, but in my firm's portfolios, I try to prepare for both outcomes.

What Zone Are You In?

What is the role that interest rates and inflation play in stock market cycles? The conventional wisdom says that low interest rates lead to high P/Es and high interest rates lead to low P/Es. I believe that conventional wisdom is too simplistic. Instead of following conventional thinking, let's look at the world through a different lens in Exhibit 3.3, which is divided into three zones. (In the discussion that follows I'll use short-term *interest rates* and *inflation* interchangeably, as they are closely related.)

- *The Dead Zone of Deflation*—Interest rates and inflation wander into this zone when there is a significant risk of deflation.
- *The Zone of Peace*—When interest rates and inflation are in the normal state.
- *The Dead Zone of Inflation*—When interest rates are above the norm, investors become concerned

Exhibit 3.3   Inflation, Interest Rates, and P/Es

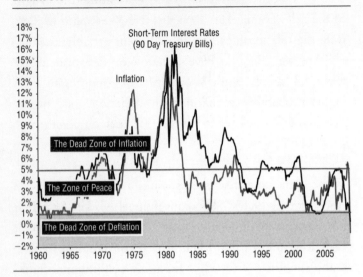

about high inflation, as they should, since inflation erodes real returns from stocks. The interest rate is a significant part of the *discount rate* investors use to discount future cash flows. A higher discount rate means future cash flows are worth less today, thus lower P/Es (this is in line with conventional wisdom).

John Maynard Keynes once said, "I'd rather be vaguely right than precisely wrong." The precision of this zoning is on the vaguely right side.

When inflation falls below a certain level, let's say 1 percent, and we enter the Dead Zone of Deflation, investors become concerned that we'll slip into deflation—a prolonged decrease in prices. Deflation brings very different risks to the table: It drives corporate revenues down while costs, which are often fixed, don't go down. Corporations start losing money; some go bankrupt. Also, unlike with inflation, the Federal Reserve has few weapons to fight deflation; thus companies are for the most part on their own.

Though the discount rate used in discounted future cash flows benefits from low interest rates, the risk premium, an integral part of that equation, skyrockets. This to some degree explains why the Japanese market's P/E collapsed—it declined from the mid-60s to the mid-teens over the last 20 years, while interest rates declined from high single digits to almost zero. Low interest rates were a product of a very sick economy—not of strength.

Movements between these zones are very important, too. Ed Easterling, in his wonderful book *Unexpected Returns* (Cypress Press, 2005), makes this point: Movements towards stability (toward the Zone of Peace from the Dead Zones of Inflation and Deflation) are very positive for P/Es, while movements away from stability (the Zone of Peace) are negative for P/Es.

Interest rates/inflation play a secondary role in stock market cycles, while human psychology dominates that game. Interest rates and inflation are ultimately responsible for where a market cycle will settle in its end game. For instance, if in the mid-1990s interest rates had not resided in the lower part of the Zone of Peace (at very low levels), but had hovered around 8 to 9 percent instead, in the Dead Zone of Inflation, the secular bull market would have ended sooner and at a lower P/E—in the low twenties instead of the low thirties. Also, if interest rates/inflation had been in the low single digits rather than double digits in the late 1970s, the 1966–1982 sideways market might have ended sooner and at a higher P/E.

Both high inflation and deflation will compress the final destination P/E, thus prolonging the length of the tracks that lead to the final P/E. However, and this is very important, inflation will increase nominal earnings growth—its speed—thus shortening the time the train will spend on the track. Conversely, deflation will decrease the nominal growth rate and thus prolong the journey. It is bad for stocks twice.

Dividends Get No Respect

If I were a dividend, I'd fire my PR agent for sure. I'd be jealous and feel neglected because stock prices get a lot more attention than they deserve. Dividends deposited into a brokerage account don't make headlines. The only time dividends get any attention is when they get cut because dividend cuts (or omissions) often go hand-in-hand with stock price declines. The stock is a victim; the dividend is the bad guy. But if I were a dividend I'd be more upset because I never get the credit I deserve; over the past hundred-plus years, dividends delivered close to half of all stock market returns.

Think about that. If you were fortunate enough to be alive over the past hundred-plus years and you had both your easy and your hard-earned money invested in the stock market, half of your returns came from dividends. Half! It gets more interesting: During the last three sideways markets, dividends were responsible for over 90 percent of stock market returns.

Not to get too algebraic here, but dividend yield is a function of two factors: dividend payout and stock market valuations. Dividend payout is the percentage of earnings corporate boards decide to share with investors. During the last century dividend payout was about 60 percent of earnings; however, from the mid-1990s to the mid-2000s it declined to about 30 percent as managements favored stock buybacks over dividend payments. From 2008 to 2009 dividend payouts went back to about 60 percent, but before you start celebrating you need to understand one little detail: That only happened because earnings during the Great Recession collapsed faster than dividends were cut. Based on more normalized earnings, the dividend payout ratio is still very low by historical standards.

To understand how valuation impacts dividend yield, we need to meet the P/E's inverse cousin, earnings yield (E/P) which is earnings divided by price. Let's assume that we have company A and company B. Both companies trade at $100 and pay out 60 percent of their earnings, but company A and company B earn $10 and $1, respectively. Company A trades at a P/E of 10 ($100 price divided by $10 earnings) and has an earnings yield (E/P) of 10 percent, while company B trades at a P/E of 100 ($100 price divided by $1 of earnings) and has an earnings yield of 1 percent. Since both pay out the same 60 percent of their earnings, the dividend yields of A and B are 6 and 0.6 percent, respectively.

Current dividend yield of the S&P 500 is only 2 percent, less than half of what stocks yielded on average over the past century. Historically, sideways markets ended when the dividend yield was between 5 and 6 percent. But what is important is that yields are now low not just because of low dividend payout ratio. Even if we were to apply a 60 percent dividend payout ratio to the $60 earnings S&P 500 stocks are expected to make in 2010, they would still yield only 3.2 percent (as of August 2010). As much as we want to blame the payout ratio, it is only partly at fault for low dividend yield; the valuation (high P/E or low E/P) is as much or even more at fault for low dividend yields.

So here is another point that we'll address in greater detail further on: Since dividends were over 90 percent of total returns during past sideways markets, do you really want to own a broad market index (such as the S&P 500) so that 2 percent becomes 90 percent of your return?

The only thing we know about the future is that it will be different.

—*Peter Drucker*

No Touch and Go

I bought a T-shirt for my wife for Mother's Day at the gift shop at Centennial Airport in Colorado. It features a picture of a Cessna airplane, and the text below it reads "No Touch and Go." This term refers to a maneuver performed when a pilot is learning to fly a plane. It involves touching down on a runway and taking off again without coming to a full stop.

Sideways markets usually don't do touch and go. They don't just touch below-average valuations and then zoom back up. Instead, they spend about half their time parked on the ground, at below-average levels, and only then do they embark on the bull market journey. In the past they typically landed in the below-average zone, and then the P/E just taxied and bounced around, driven by stock prices and, to lesser degree, earnings volatility.

Being "in Stocks" Is Not Good Enough; What Stocks You Own Matters!

During secular bull markets a well-dressed, blindfolded monkey throwing a dart at the *Wall Street Journal* stock tables could have picked a portfolio of 100 stocks that would do better than bonds. Take a look at Exhibit 3.4, which shows real (after inflation) performance of stocks, long-term bonds, and Treasury bills during the 1982–2000 bull market. Bonds seriously underperformed during that time, so being in stocks as an asset class—be it an index fund or a large basket of stocks—was the way to go.

Sideways markets are a very different story. Historically, stock performance has been only slightly better and sometimes marginally worse than bonds. As you see in Exhibit 3.5, during the 1966–1982 sideways market, stocks barely outperformed long-term bonds and were beaten by Treasury bills. Depending on what interest rates and inflation do over the next decade, broad market indexes may or may not be a superior investment

Exhibit 3.4   Stocks Crash Bonds and T-Bills

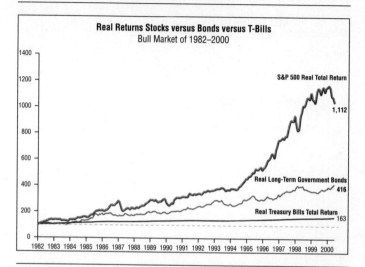

Real Returns Stocks versus Bonds versus T-Bills
Bull Market of 1982–2000

S&P 500 Real Total Return — 1,112

Real Long-Term Government Bonds — 416

Real Treasury Bills Total Return — 163

Source: Active Value Investing by Vitaliy Katsenelson (John Wiley & Sons, 2007, page 70). Reprinted with permission of John Wiley & Sons, Inc.

Data sources: Treasury bills and bonds—Ibbotson; CPI and Stocks (S&P 500)—Robert J. Shiller. Exhibits sourced Ibbotson Associates are from: *Stocks, Bonds, Bills and Inflation 2007 Classic Edition Yearbook.* © 2010 Morningstar. All rights reserved. Used with permission. Copies of the *Yearbook* may be acquired directly from Morningstar. For more information, please visit www.morningstar.com.

to bonds, as P/E expansion will not be a source of stock returns.

The good news is that there are bright spots. The *right* stocks will rule in sideways markets! In bull markets, all stocks dominate bonds. Owning a broad market

Exhibit 3.5   Stocks Are Not Better Than "Cash"

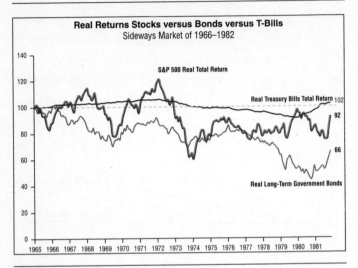

Source: Active Value Investing by Vitaliy Katsenelson (John Wiley & Sons, 2007, page 68).
Reprinted with permission of John Wiley & Sons, Inc.

Data sources: Treasury bills and bonds—Ibbotson; CPI and Stocks (S & P 500)—Robert
J. Shiller. Exhibits sourced Ibbotson Associates are from: *Stocks, Bonds, Bills and Inflation
2007 Classic Edition Yearbook.* © 2010 Morningstar. All rights reserved. Used with permission.
Copies of the *Yearbook* may be acquired directly from Morningstar. For more information,
please visit www.morningstar.com.

index—a passive buy-and-hold strategy—does wonders.
During sideways markets, *all* stocks don't dominate fixed
income instruments; only the right stocks do. A finely
tuned, actively managed portfolio will have the best shot
at outperforming bonds and short-term securities over the
course of a sideways market. Rigorous stock selection and

a disciplined buy-and-sell strategy must be used to make money in this low-return environment.

The opportunity cost of being invested in fixed income instruments as opposed to average quality stocks is much lower in a sideways market than in a bull market. Don't own stocks just to be invested. In the absence of attractive equity investments—the right stocks—fixed-income instruments (or cash) are viable alternatives to an "average" stock.

What is the right stock? The next part of the book will tell you just that!

Chapter Four

Tevye Was a Rich Man

~

The Quintessential Value Investor

I'D LIKE TO INTRODUCE YOU TO MY HERO, Tevye the Milkman. Didn't read about him in your investing books? Tevye came to life in the stories of Shalom Aleichem, and later to the silver screen in the musical *Fiddler on the Roof*.

Tevye is my hero not just because he is a font of worldly wisdom, or because he can sing, or because he is a great and kind father, or because he romances the memories of my ancestors. I honor Tevye because he is a *pragmatic value investor*.

Tevye lives in a small village in eastern Europe; he is a farmer and a milkman. He may not be familiar with the maxim that the value of any asset is the present value of the asset's future cash flows, but that doesn't prevent him from applying these principles.

Tevye's story highlights what value investing is all about: analyzing an asset be it a cow, a stock, or a bond by assessing its risk; valuing it or figuring out what it is worth; and calculating a suitable purchase price. If an asset trades at the desired price or below it, you buy it; if not, you wait patiently until it gets to your target price. That's it!

Unfortunately, market noise often deflects us off this simple path, but it really is that simple. I often think about Tevye to keep my focus amid the daily noise.

Meet Our Hero

Tevye needs to buy a young cow. He plans to name her Golde, after his first wife. Based on his previous experience, he expects Golde to produce about 2,500 gallons of milk a year, bringing him about $3,000 in revenues a year. After paying for a barn, high-quality feed, stud fees, top-notch veterinary services, his otherwise unemployed nephew to take care of and milk Golde, and finally, taxes, he expects to pocket about $1,000 a year from the milk (see Exhibit 4.1).

Exhibit 4.1   What Is Golde Worth?

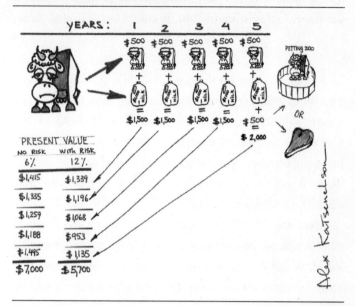

Source: *Active Value Investing* by Vitaliy Katsenelson (John Wiley & Sons, 2007, page 121). Reprinted with permission of John Wiley & Sons, Inc.

Tevye further expects Golde to rear a calf every year (fairly usual for cows), which Tevye will sell at a livestock auction for $500 (after tax). After five years of hard work Golde's milk production will likely fall off, and Tevye can then sell 700-pound Golde to his friend the butcher for $500. For the sake of those who don't want to see Golde slaughtered, he might sell her to a local petting zoo—he is a kind man, after all. Tevye is not aware of it, but that final goodbye, Golde's liquidation, is called her terminal value.

What's She Worth?

Tevye believes that, at the most, Golde will be worth about $8,000 to him. He figures that between milk ($1,000) and a calf ($500) she will generate cash flow of about $1,500 a year for five years—that is, $7,500 plus another $500 from the butcher or petting zoo at the end of year five. So Tevye figures that it doesn't make sense to pay more than $8,000 for Golde.

But, the $8,000 he hopes to receive over the five-year period will not be the same as the $8,000 he pays today—a lot of things can happen in five years, including inflation and opportunities for Tevye to spend his money elsewhere; that is, opportunity cost.

Tevye's son-in-law, a banker, finds out that Tevye is contemplating buying Golde. Wanting to win his father-in-law's heart, he offers (on behalf of the bank he works for) to finance Golde's future cash flows by giving Tevye a lump sum of $7,000 today. In exchange, Tevye must agree to pay the bank $1,500 a year for five years and an additional $500 at the end of year five from selling Golde. In other words, the son-in-law's bank will finance Golde's purchase at 6 percent a year (or Tevye can deposit in the bank at 6 percent a year if he wishes to do so).

Tevye didn't really think he needed the financing, but his son-in-law gave him an important insight: If Tevye could predict and forecast Golde's cash flows with absolute certainty, taking all the risk out of the transaction, then he could accept his son-in-law's offer and buy Golde at the livestock auction for $7,000 at the most. But why bother buying Golde for $7,000? He could just give the money to his son-in-law and let earning 6 percent a year be his son-in-law's problem.

If Tevye bought Golde for $7,000, he would be compensated for inflation and opportunity cost but not for risk, and there was plenty of it.

- Golde could get sick.
- Feed prices could skyrocket, while Tevye might not be able to raise prices for his milk to offset the cost, and thus selling milk could turn into a profitless endeavor.
- Milk prices could decline due to competition from farmers across the pond.
- The "other" milk could start stealing shelf space from "real" milk in the local supermarket. (Tevye has never had much respect for soy milk, which he called soy juice. He told his daughters, "When you find an udder on a soybean, I'll call it milk.")

- Taxes could increase at the whim of people he doesn't know in order to finance things that Tevye does not really understand or care about.

Tevye's gut and experience are telling him he should at least demand double the riskless rate of 6 percent that his son-in-law is offering him and require a 12 percent rate of return for Golde's risky cash flows. This would bring Golde's fair value (also called intrinsic value) to about $5,700. In other words, instead of discounting Golde's cash flows (bringing future cash flows to today's value) at 6 percent—as his son-in-law did when he offered Tevye $7,000—Tevye thinks he should use 12 percent, as is shown in Exhibit 4.1. Some may say that would be asking for a 6 percent premium to a risk-free rate of 6 percent.

If Tevye bought Golde for $5,700 he would be compensated for inflation, opportunity cost, and the risks that come with owning a cow.

Of course, unpredictability of future cash flows could always turn in his favor. Milk prices might increase, feed prices and taxes could decline, beef prices could climb, Golde could turn out to be a super cow and produce a lot more milk than anticipated, or the petting zoo could pay several times what he expected for Golde. However, his years of experience have taught him to hope for the best and prepare for the worst. If the future turns out brighter than he expects, that will be a nice bonus and he will be able to install indoor plumbing in his house.

Factoring In Risk

———————— ∼ ————————

The margin of safety is dependent on the price paid. It will be large at one price, small at some other price, and nonexistent at some higher price.
—*Benjamin Graham,* The Intelligent Investor

Tevye never met Benjamin Graham, nor did he read his book *The Intelligent Investor;* he never heard of the "margin of safety"—buying stocks at a discount to fair value—that Benjamin Graham popularized in his writings. However, Tevye had several daughters' weddings to pay for, and this transformed him into a cautious farmer. He thought if he bought something at fair value (Golde at $5,700 would be fairly valued after factoring in the risk, as we have seen), then he'd have little margin for being wrong. Even if his forecasts were right on the money, there were still many variables that he could not control or forecast. He knew that forecasts were rarely right on the money and things usually went more wrong than right.

Exhibit 4.2   Golde's Absolute Valuation Stats

Sum of all Golde's cash flows	$8,000
Fair value if cash flows discounted at 6% required "riskless" rate of return	$7,000
Tevye's perception of fair value if cash flows discounted at 12% "risky" required rate	$5,700
Golde's purchase price (with 25% margin of safety)	$4,300

Source: *Active Value Investing* by Vitaliy Katsenelson (John Wiley & Sons, 2007, page 122). Reprinted with permission of John Wiley & Sons, Inc.

Discounting Golde's cash flows using the 12 percent risky rate provided Tevye some buffer for being wrong (see Exhibit 4.2). The 6 percent risk premium provided a $1,300 risk premium buffer (the difference between $7,000 and $5,700). However, if Golde was purchased at fair value of $5,700 and cash flows came in below Tevye's estimates, he would not be fully compensated for the risk taken. For this reason, he needed to buy Golde with a margin of safety.

He needed a margin of safety to protect him for two reasons:

1. If things turned out as expected or better, then he would have made an extra return from buying Golde below estimated fair value of $5,700. For instance, if he purchased Golde at $4,300, about a 25 percent margin of safety, and all assumptions played out as he expected, then in addition to earning a 12 percent

annual rate of return Tevye would make $1,400
from the margin of safety.

2. More important, if Tevye made a mistake in forecasting future cash flows, or some of the risks surfaced and impacted cash flows, he'd have a margin
of safety to fall back on. At a 25 percent margin
of safety, cash flows could be off by $1,400 and he
still would make his 12 percent annual rate of
return.

With these thoughts, Tevye went to the livestock auction looking for his Golde.

At the Livestock Auction

Tevye did not buy Golde on the first day of the auction.
The weather was sunny, his fellow farmers were excited
about the prospects of the cattle market, and the bidding
for cows went too high—many sold above their intrinsic
value. Many farmers got caught up in the excitement, for-
got they were farmers, and bought cows like crazy, ignoring expected cash flows and hoping other farmers would
buy these cows at even higher prices tomorrow.

The second day was more productive than the first,
but still Tevye did not buy his Golde. The prices were still
too high, but instead of obsessing over the market action
and prices, Tevye did additional research on the cows that

were available for sale. He identified the best of breed, the ones that would be less susceptible to getting sick and had the potential to surprise him with their milk production.

The third day was Tevye's day—the day when he bought his Golde. It was a rainy day, and cattle prices reflected the weather; they declined. Many disappointed farmers who had just bought cows at prices above their intrinsic values with the hope of selling them at a profit now were selling them at any price, just to recover some of their investment. In addition all of this coincided with the liquor store next door having a huge sale, and many disenchanted farmers went to take advantage of it.

Tevye found his Golde. She was not the star of the show, but she was definitely best of breed; she met all Tevye's stringent quality criteria, and the best part was, Tevye bought her with a 25-percent margin of safety to her intrinsic value—he paid only $4,300!

The Final Tally

Without giving it a second thought, Tevye used a discounted cash-flow model to analyze Golde's purchase. He estimated the drivers of value:

- The revenues—milk, calves, and beef (or proceeds from selling Golde to a petting zoo)—she would produce over the years.

- The costs associated with taking care of his favorite cow, which had all the personality traits of his first wife (calm, cooperative, low-maintenance).
- Her longevity—the longer Golde can keep producing high-quality milk, the more valuable she becomes. (Note that the same logic applies to valuing stocks. The more durable a company's competitive advantage, the further and the more confidence you'll have in projecting its cash flows forward, and the further ahead you can forecast its cash flows, the more valuable is the company.)
- The external risk factors—the whims of consumer demand, taxes, political risks, regulation of the dairy industry, and so on.

Estimating all these creators (and possible destroyers) of value was an immensely important mental exercise, as it kept Tevye in the boots of a farmer instead of the fickle shoes of a speculator.

He believed that if, at the livestock auction on day one, his fellow farmers had been making their decisions based on expected cash flows from the cows, they would not have been buying cows as if milk were about to become the new vodka. Discounted cash-flow analysis would have cooled down the euphoria that came with a sunny day and rising cattle prices, and it would have kept the farmers from turning into speculators.

This process of analyzing and determining Golde's worth radiated a false appearance of precision, but for Tevye it was anything but precise. He knew that any time you use even simple math, the false appearance of precision is hard to avoid. For Tevye it was a framework of thinking about return and risk; it allowed him to bring in his real-world experience and quantify his assumptions. The process also helped him understand which creators and destroyers had the most potential impact on Golde's value.

If Tevye found a cow whose character he liked but whose cash flows he was less certain of—maybe there was a history of illness in its bloodline, or it appeared to lack the stamina of his Golde—he'd either increase the discount rate (maybe using 15 percent instead of 12) or increase the required margin of safety (perhaps from 25 percent to 40 percent).

External (not cow-specific) factors could also force Tevye to rethink his discount rate or margin of safety. Every so often a new government made promises to farmers that it could not keep, and later it had to raise taxes or print money to keep these promises. Higher taxes reduced his profits in a very apparent way, while high inflation corroded his profits in a more subtle way; or, as Tevye's favorite thinker, Yogi Berra, put it, "A nickel ain't worth a dime anymore." Either way, if Tevye had a feeling that the current government was making promises it could not keep, he would start raising his required rate of return or margin of safety, proactively.

Tevye loved his overeducated son-in-law, the banker, insofar as he provided for his daughter, but Tevye was fairly certain that the banker's fancy valuation models that were based on elegant formulas with Greek symbols and provided exquisitely precise answers lacked common sense.

Price to "Anything"

Tevye used some shortcuts to assist him in purchasing Golde. These were the "price to anything" ratios (more accurately, price divided by anything), where anything could be earnings, cash flow, revenues, gallons of milk, or anything else! His son-in-law called them relative valuation tools, as they established a relative value link between a price and a value creator ("anything").

Relative valuation tools were not an intuitive to Tevye at first, but after using them for a while he learned to appreciate their simplicity and ease of use.

After a while, price-to-cash flow started to appeal to Tevye's intuitive sense. As shown in Exhibit 4.3, at $5,700 (Golde's fair value in his estimate), he would have paid 3.8 times Golde's annual cash flows of $1,500 ($5,700 divided by $1,500), and so it would take him just a bit less than four years to break even on Golde's purchase.

Exhibit 4.3   Golde's and Similar Cows Relative Valuation Stats

	Price to Cash Flows
Highest price over previous five years: $12,000	3.8 times
Young farmer purchased Golde-like cow for $10,500	8 times
Golde's fair price according to Tevye: $5,700	3.8 times
Golde's purchase price (with 25% margin of safety): $4,300	2.9 times
Lowest price over previous five years: $4,050	2.7 times

Source: Active Value Investing by Vitaliy Katsenelson (John Wiley & Sons, 2007, page 126). Reprinted with permission of John Wiley & Sons, Inc.

Whereas estimating and discounting Golde's cash flows provided Tevye with an insight into Golde's value in absolute terms, relative valuation tools provided a relative assessment for pricing value creators when considering Golde's history or in relation to the valuation of other cows. Tevye found that often "price to anything" measures were an adequate shortcut to figure out the appropriate price of a cow.

Despite the provinciality of Tevye's livestock auction, farmers still had to disclose the cash flows and revenues that their cows generated in previous years in accordance with rules of the Cow Exchange Commission (CEC). The CEC checked the accuracy of farmers' claims, and those who had the audacity to deceive their fellow farmers were publicly whipped.

From his wealth of experience, Tevye knew that at 3.8 times cash flows a typical two-year-old cow (and Golde had just turned two) was fairly valued. A quick look at historical price-to-cash flow ratios confirmed that on average a cow of Golde's stature changed hands at about 4 times cash flows. Also, over the previous five years, similar cows changed hands at as low as 2.7 times cash flows (putting a price tag of $4,050 on Golde), and went as high as 8 times (putting a $12,000 price tag on her). In Tevye's estimation, at 8 times cash flows ($12,000 price tag), Golde would change hands at a higher value than the sum of all the cash flows she could possibly produce for her owner over her entire productive life ($8,000).

Bingo! Tevye had an epiphany. He saw one of the greatest limitations of "price to anything" measures: In the heat of the moment these measures can lose their meaning for farmers and turn them into irrational speculators.

The Day Tevye Bought His Golde

On day two at the livestock auction, Tevye overheard two farmers having an interesting conversation. The younger one argued that at 7 times cash flows ($10,500) the cow he had his eye on was a great buy, as only yesterday (on day one) she had demanded as much as 8 times cash flows. The other farmer, substantially older than the first, who had experience and common sense written all over his wrinkled face (just like Tevye), said:

Son, just because one fool found a bigger fool to buy a cow for a ridiculous price doesn't mean that's what the cow is worth. Knowing what happened in the past doesn't tell us what will happen tomorrow. After the dust settles and everybody comes down from all the excitement, prices will swing back to their true level. How long will that take? Well, it may or may not take a while; the answer will be obvious to us only after the fact. That's why I stop bidding on sunny days when everybody's got a smile on their face. True value gets real hard to peg on days like that. And of this I'm certain: The cash flows that this cow will bring for its owner in the future don't support the 7 times cash-flow multiple that she's trading for at the moment.

The younger farmer shrugged and bought a Golde-like cow anyway, expecting to sell it the next day (day three) at a higher price. As the older farmer predicted, the dust did settle, and it didn't take long at all. In fact, it settled the very next morning.

Tevye believed that the past price-to-cash flow ratio had its advantages, as it showed the valuation road on which Golde had traveled in the past. However, don't forget that he was a cautious fellow. He believed that knowing the past is helpful, but he understood that the valuation road that farmers will take cows down in the future might not be at all like the roads already traveled.

And as it turned out, the price-to-cash flow ratio quickly helped Tevye to identify undervalued cows at the livestock auction. In addition, when farmers started to panic and cattle prices began to plummet, he could without difficulty gauge the level of cheapness of the overall cattle market. He objectively determined the required margin of safety for Golde—25 percent—and figured that he wanted to buy Golde at about 2.9 times cash flows (3.8, the fair value price-to-cash flow, reduced by a 25-percent margin of safety). Then he just waited for prices to drop and bought his Golde.

Tevye didn't buy Golde at the lowest possible price, but he bought her at a significant discount to her intrinsic value. Maybe if he had waited a little longer he could have gotten her a bit cheaper, but Tevye didn't mind, because he knew he'd bought a great cow at a great price. Besides, trying to outsmart the auction by scraping the bottom had emotional appeal but little practical value. It might have let him brag to his neighbors about how smart he was, but that was not Tevye. The bragging rights meant little to him, since they wouldn't help him to pay for his daughters' weddings; and after all, that is what this purchase was about.

Chapter Five

What We Can Learn from Gamblers

~

Investment Success Comes from Process

SEVERAL YEARS AGO ON A BUSINESS TRIP, I went to a casino to play blackjack. Aware that the odds were stacked against me, I set a $40 limit on how much I was willing to lose. Wanting to get as much mileage out of my $40 as possible, I found a table with the smallest minimum bet requirement. My thinking was that the cheaper the hands I played, the more time it would take for the casino's advantage to catch up with me and take my money.

I joined a table that was dominated by a rowdy, half-drunken fellow who told me several times that it was his payday (literally: He was holding a stack of $100 bills in his hand) and that he was winning. I played by the book. But that didn't seem to matter—luck wasn't on my side. The rowdy guy was making every wrong move. He would ask for an extra card when he had a hard 18 while the dealer showed 6. The next card he drew would be a 3, giving him 21. Then the dealer would get a 10 and then a 2 (on top of the 6 that already showed), leaving him with 18. The rowdy guy barely paid attention to the cards. He was more interested in saying "Hit me."

Every "right" decision I made turned into a losing bet, while every "wrong" decision he made turned into a winner. His stack of chips was growing while mine was dwindling. His loud behavior and consistent winnings attracted several observers. Some were making comments such as "This guy is good." Nobody paid attention to me—I was not loud and I was losing.

The rowdy guy had no process in place. He was just making half-drunken bets that had statistical improbabilities of success. And he was winning—at least for a while. I was armed with statistics, making every bet to maximize my chances of winning (or rather to minimize my losses—the odds were still against me), but I was on the losing side of the game.

After a couple of hours, and after consuming more of the free alcohol, my rowdy companion was increasing the size of his bets with every successful hand. Then the law of large numbers caught up with him. He gave up all his winnings and his paycheck as well; two weeks of hard work sadly but predictably went into the casino's coffers. I was down to a couple of dollars at one point, but then my luck changed and I won the bulk of my money back.

What is the lesson here? Spend more time focusing on the process than on the end results. If it were not for randomness, every decision we make would be right or wrong based solely on the outcome. If that were the case, the process could be judged solely on the end result. But randomness is as constantly present in investing as it is in gambling. Although we are drawn to judge our decisions and those of others on their outcomes, it is dangerous to do so. Randomness may teach us the wrong lessons.

--- ≈ ---

Any time you make a bet with the best of it, where the odds are in your favor, you have earned something on that bet, whether you actually win or lose the bet. By the same token, when you make a bet with the worst of it, where the odds are not in your favor, you have lost something, whether you actually win or lose the bet.
—*David Sklansky,* The Theory of Poker

The Gambler in All of Us

Over a lifetime, active investors will make hundreds, often thousands, of investment decisions. Not all of those will work out for the better. Some will lose money and some will make us money. As humans we tend to focus on the outcome of the decision rather than on the process. On a behavioral level, this makes sense. The outcome is binary to us—good or bad, which we can observe with ease. But the process is more complex and is often hidden from us.

One of two things, and sometimes a bit of both, unite great investors: process and luck (randomness). Unfortunately, there is not much we can learn from randomness, as it has no predictive power. But the process is something we should study and learn from. To be a successful investor, what you need is a successful process and the ability and mental strength to stick to it.

It is important to realize the duality of definition (at least as it applies to investing) of the word *discipline*:

1. A system of rules, or a systematic method.
2. Control obtained by enforcing compliance.

The first definition can be interchangeably used with *process*—a system of rules. The second is really about being in control and sticking to the process. To avoid confusing the issue with phrases like "disciplined discipline," for the first meaning of discipline I'll use the word *process*, and for the second, *discipline*.

My rowdy gambling companion did not have a process, unless you call yelling "Hit me" one. He had no process to be disciplined to, unless ordering free beer twice an hour counts as a discipline. Even if he won that day, in the long run, unless the gods of randomness decided to play a cruel joke, after playing for many hours he'd have no chance of succeeding (defined here as minimizing your losses)—because he had neither a process nor a discipline.

Hold 'Em and Fold 'Em Like Tevye

The story about my hero Tevye should have put you into the state of mind of a value investor, and I hope my gambling adventure emphasized the importance of process (in investing as well as in gambling). Now it's time for the "how to" portion of the book: We are about to dive into the investment process I've developed specifically for sideways markets, Active Value Investing. The less ambiguous your investment process, the more likely you'll have the discipline to stick to it. Chapters 6 through 8 will cover the Quality, Valuation, and Growth framework, which will add clarity to your stock analysis, and then Chapter 9 will pull all three together. Chapters 9 through 17 will provide a solid strategy of execution—the buy and sell process.

Chapter Six

Brought to You by the Letter "Q" (for Quality)

DON'T LOSE MONEY.

This advice sounds as banal as the slew of dos and don'ts (mostly don'ts) we get from parents as teenagers—don't speed, don't stay up late at night, don't drink and drive, use . . . I didn't say they were useless, just banal. So keeping that in mind, I am still going to say don't lose money during sideways markets. Not that you should go out of your way to lose money during bull markets, of course not; but in a rising market it's much easier to get back any losses you may suffer along the way. During a sideways market, the bull market tailwind that helps us make up losses turns into a tough headwind that makes it significantly more difficult to make up for losses. The QVG framework that I've developed and am about to introduce to you will help you to achieve this banal but all-important goal. Let's start with the first in QVG, letter Q—Quality.

**Quality is remembered long after
the price is forgotten.**

—Gucci family slogan

A high-quality company is one that is able to maintain, or even to increase, its earnings power over an extended period of time, let's say 10 or 20 years. It's one that is able to emerge from an economic hurricane as strong as it entered it (or even stronger). Now that we know what a quality company is on the surface, let's take a peek at its components.

The Barbed Wire Fence

A business that can put money to work and earn a high return (a high return on capital) will draw new competition, as the competitors will look at high returns the way hummingbirds look at sugar water—they'll want some of that. Unless a business has a sustainable competitive advantage—a metaphorical electrical or barbed-wire fence with sharp spikes projecting from its top—competitors will march in and (depending on the nature of the company's product or service) force it to lower prices, give up some of its volume, invest heavily in advertising or R&D in some combination or another. After the dust settles, the company's return on capital will have declined and so too its profits. The higher the voltage flows through this fence or the sharper the spikes, the less likely competitors will be able to do this.

Sustainable competitive advantage may come from different sources, such as strong brands, high barriers to entry, patent protection, or other factors that allow a company to have a leg up against competitive threats. Competitive advantage is the one criterion on which you should not be willing to compromise.

Companies that have a history of producing a high return on capital have (in most cases) a competitive advantage that allows them to maintain those returns. If the competitive advantage remains intact, then high return on capital is likely to persist going forward.

Return on capital is one of two main ingredients in the earnings growth formula. The higher the return on invested capital, the less equity or debt a company must issue to grow. Assuming a company has growth opportunities—the second main ingredient in the growth formula—a company with high return on capital is able to grow based on internally generated funds. This means higher earnings growth with less risk. Issuance of new stock means that the same earnings pie has to be divided into smaller pieces (more shares outstanding), which dilutes returns and lowers the dividend per share. Issuance of debt adds another expense line on the income statement and increases the company's risk.

Not All Brands Are Created Equal

Strong brands often provide a competitive advantage and deter new entrants from stepping into the marketplace. However, not all brands are created equal, and some brands only provide the right to compete but not the right to charge premium prices. In 2004 I was analyzing Sara Lee Corporation. At the time this company owned Jimmy Dean, Hillshire Farm, Ball Park, L'eggs, Hanes (underwear), and many other respectable brands. You'd think these strong brands would command higher pricing and thus allow the company to raise prices without a substantial impact on demand. That was not the case.

Every time the company tried to raise prices for its hot dogs, sausages, or underwear (often in an attempt to pass higher commodity prices on to the consumer), demand dropped substantially. Consumers did not stop eating hot dogs or sausages (that would be un-American), or wearing underwear (that would just be wrong); they simply switched to other brands.

Consumers are overwhelmed by the abundance of brands in stores. Any innovation by one strong-brand company is quickly copied by another one with a similar strong brand identity.

A strong, well-known consumer brand doesn't always guarantee a higher selling price or higher margin, but it does help in securing shelf space and a selling price higher than that of a generic store brand. In the case of Sara Lee (and this is also true for many other companies), its strong brands may have prevented new entrants from barging into the industry, but its brand strength did not protect it from incumbent "high-branded" competitors undermining its profit margins.

I am not dismissing the importance of brands, but rather issuing a warning: Just because a company has a well-known, respected brand, you cannot assume that the brand will bring a sustainable competitive advantage to the table.

The Power of Free Cash Flows

When Tevye was valuing Golde he did not pay close attention to earnings; he focused on cash flows. His thought was, you cannot spend earnings; the grocery store around the corner doesn't accept earnings as payment for bread but never seems to have a problem with cash. Dividends are paid and stock is bought back with cash, not earnings. Earnings are mired in accounting assumptions and skillfully played by ambitious management in a quest to meet Wall Street's consensus estimates. Though cash flows are more volatile than earnings in the short run, they tell a truer story of a company's profitability.

When I say cash flows, I really mean free cash flows—the cash left after a company pays its expenses, such as salaries, taxes, inventory, interest, management's country club memberships, various other yearly expenses, and all other expenses required for future growth, such as investment in fixed assets (building new factories and so on).

Companies with significant free cash flows that are managed by smart, shareholder-oriented management will be able to take advantage of volatility in sideways markets and thus create additional shareholder value through appropriate stock buybacks (at a time when the company's stock is cheap). Significant reduction of share count results in higher earnings and an increase in dividends per share, thus acting as a flotation buoy under the stock.

But benefits from free cash flows don't stop there. Companies that generate significant free cash flows usually don't require a lot of capital (i.e., large investments in property, plant, and equipment, and so on). This often leads to a higher return on capital and greater earnings growth. It also gives a company financial independence from the outside financial world, as free cash flows allow the company to finance its business internally. When the economy is humming along, companies can easily issue stock or borrow money by issuing bonds or taking out bank loans. At such times self-reliance on internal financing may go unnoticed (and not be priced into a stock). However, during tough times, high free cash flows and the ability to finance internally will separate the survivors from the has-beens.

In times of economic difficulty or in a crisis, the buying power of cash increases exponentially. For example, Pfizer, the largest pharmaceutical company in the world, was able to buy (more like steal) Wyeth, another large pharmaceutical company, in the midst of a financial crisis, at 13 times earnings. After considering cost savings from operating redundancies, Pfizer paid closer to 10 times earnings—an incredibly low price considering that in the past these types of transactions were done at multiples of closer to 20 times or higher.

Not All Capital Expenditures Are Created Equal

In the free cash flow definition there is almost no quarrel over what constitutes operating cash flow: It is net income adjusted for all noncash (mainly depreciation and amortization) and operation-related balance sheet items (mainly inventories, accounts receivable, and accounts payable). However, capital expenditure levels may understate or overstate company free cash flows, as not all capital expenditures are created equal. An important distinction between investment in future growth and maintenance-capital expenditures often goes unnoticed.

Maintenance-capital expenditures are investments required for a company to maintain its current sales level. A semiconductor company, for instance, has to constantly upgrade its factory just to maintain current sales, since technology and manufacturing processes are constantly evolving. Oil companies, too, have to spend billions of dollars every year just to replenish depleting oil wells (reserves). If they stop looking for new oil, over time they'll deplete their reserves and go out of business. To identify maintenance-capital expenditures, ask yourself a question: What would happen to a company's sales if it stopped investing in fixed assets? If its sales would be expected to decline over time, as would happen to semiconductor and oil companies, then you have uncovered maintenance-capital expenditures, all other things being equal.

Future-growth capital expenditures are investments necessary for a company to grow its sales, such as a retailer building new stores or a shipbuilder expanding its ship-yard. If a company stopped making growth-capital expen-ditures, all other things being equal, its sales would stop growing but not decline.

Why is it important to distinguish among capital expenditures? We live in a finite world where infinite above-average growth of earnings (and cash flows) is not possible—a company growing at a rate substantially above industry growth would at some point become the indus-try, then the entire economy!

The larger a company becomes, the more difficult it is to grow at the same high rate. This result is as inevi-table as gravity. A company that has a high level of maintenance-capital expenditures is unlikely to generate higher free cash flows—even after it stops growing sales—since it will keep pouring money (albeit lower amounts) into fixed assets to keep existing sales from declining.

A company with low maintenance-capital expenditures will see a substantial increase in free cash flows once it stops growing sales (investing for growth), since its capi-tal expenditures will decline and free cash flows and income will rise. Its stock price is likely to suffer less rela-tive to a company with high maintenance-capital expendi-tures, since its P/E will decline less (which inevitably comes with slower growth) and be able to boost dividends and buy back stock.

This is exactly what happened to Wal-Mart, which has been decreasing the rate of new store openings in the United States since 2007. Following that move, although its operating cash flows have grown from $20 billion to $23 billion mostly driven by more efficient working-capital management and an increase in same-store sales, its free cash flows have ballooned from $5 billion to $12. A large portion of the increase was due to the decline of capital expenditures from $15 billion to $11 billion. As Wal-Mart's growth keeps slowing down, its free cash flows will be increasing.

Another important point. There is a way to capitalize on companies that have high maintenance-capital expenditures: Buy companies that sell capital equipment to them. For instance, semiconductor companies have high maintenance-capital expenditures. As we discussed, they need to constantly upgrade their factories as microprocessors keep getting faster and smaller—in general, not a great business. However, companies that sell them equipment are much more attractive businesses. The semiconductor company's high maintenance-capital expenditures turn into the equipment company's recurring revenues.

Free cash flow volatility is usually higher than volatility of net income. Annual volatility of free cash flows may send you down the wrong track. One year free cash flow may be positive, only to go negative the next year. The best way to deal with free cash flow volatility is to either average or compute cumulative operating cash flows over a several-year span and then correspondingly either reduce them by average or cumulative capital expenditures over that time period.

Analyze This

———————————— ∾ ————————————

Never pay the slightest attention to what a company president ever says about his stock.

—*Bernard Baruch*

Management should be analyzed and evaluated as meticulously as a company's balance sheet. Its comments should be filtered through your internal commonsense filter, no matter how successful management's track record is. Their pay and incentives are tied to company stock performance, creating enormous pressure to maintain a perpetually rising stock price. In fact, as long as a stock price keeps rising, managerial and operational flaws are usually overlooked by the board and shareholders, whereas a stock price decline serves as a giant perverse magnifying glass that amplifies flaws and deamplifies successes.

Management is responsible for creating and executing a company's strategy. However, above all its primary goal should be to enhance the company's long-term sustainable competitive advantage. If they do that an increase in shareholder value will follow.

The car salesman may be telling you the truth about a car but, because he has an inherent bias to sell you the car, you still don't take him at his word and you do your own research (or at least you should). The car salesman is not a bad person, but he may have a family to support. His job is to sell you *this* car, not the best car and not at the best price. What would you expect? Corporate managements in theory are held to a higher standard and thus we are more inclined to believe them than car salespeople, but their biases and incentives are not very different from these salespeople; their job is to sell you *this* stock at its *current* market price.

We need to slightly recalibrate our commonsense filters so we don't get swayed by the personality delivering the message. Executives are usually well-spoken, confident individuals—qualities required to run a company. But these qualities can overwhelm us. We need to humanize the speaker, stripping away the success, fancy title, and confidence, and removing the appearance of infallibility. Try to imagine the executive wearing a clown suit or whatever else will do the trick of eliminating the superhuman aura. Once we humanize the executive, our commonsense filters are more likely to recognize bias and adjust for it.

Though wise short-term and long-term decisions are not mutually exclusive, in order to grow a tree (a long-term investment) seeds have to be planted (immediate expense). Management faces these decisions on a daily basis and unfortunately often destroys long-term value to please the short-term junkies who populate Wall Street.

Over time, the Street's obsession with short-term goals has shifted management focus from creating long-term value for shareholders to becoming Wall Street's lap dog, trying to jump to the next level every quarter as the bar is inexorably raised by its masters.

I was surprised to hear the answer Jon Feltheimer (CEO of Lionsgate Entertainment, an independent movie studio) gave to an analyst's question on the company's conference call.

The analyst asked: "There does appear to be a move toward squeezing those windows closer together [time between when a movie comes out in the theater and on DVD]. I am wondering what the pros and cons of that are?" Feltheimer's answer: "We think 16 weeks is still about the right amount between windows. I do not think we see really compressing them much more than that. I think there are times, particularly as a public company, when you are trying to get certain revenues within your fiscal year, and you move a movie a couple of weeks, so maybe the window changes a little." (CallStreet.com, transcript of Lionsgate Entertainment Corporation's first quarter 2007 earnings call.)

In a rational, long-term value-creation world, the movie or DVD release to the public would have nothing to do with when its release falls within a quarter; it would be based on when people would likely want to see it and when the company would make the most money.

One disadvantage of being a public company is your choice of masters—your shareholders. Wall Street is short-term oriented, and it has an insatiable need to constantly grow short-term returns.

What should you do? Look for a management team that has the guts and the confidence to keep a long-term focus and to make fewer cowardly, compromising decisions that hinder a company's long-term sustainable competitive advantage merely to serve a hungry master.

How Good Is Management at Spending Your Money?

Never underestimate management's ability to spend (more appropriately, waste) your money so they can build larger but not necessarily better empires. The larger the company they run, the more important they feel and the bigger the paychecks they can demand from the board.

Let's take a look at Regis Corporation, which is the owner/franchisor of 13,000 hair salons worldwide—the largest hair salon company on earth. I cannot think of a simpler and more predictable business than hair salons. Like it or not, hair keeps growing. Even if we age and have fewer hairs to cut each month, more new heads with growing hair come on the scene, and they all need to be trimmed on a semiregular basis.

The costs of opening a salon are minimal (a payback in two years at the most), little inventory is required, technological changes take place only every hundred years or so, and patrons are conditioned to expect annual price increases (I am sure a haircut was a quarter a few decades ago). Despite the relative simplicity of the core business, for years Regis has been run into the ground by management's less-than-stellar capital allocation decisions.

The problem with Regis's business was that it was too good; it generated too much cash flow (no, that's not a misprint). Too much cash and incompetent management, to paraphrase P.J. O'Rourke, is like giving whiskey and car keys to teenage boys.

Over the last decade, though sales have doubled, earnings per share are up only slightly (a few percent), return on capital is down by almost half, debt is up, and share count is up 38 percent. It gets worse. Over the last decade Regis businesses brought in cumulatively $1,852 million of operating cash flows, of which $961 million was spent on capital expenditures. In other words, Regis had free cash flows of $891 million. Regis graciously paid $62 million in dividends to shareholders, thus fully discretionary free cash flows, after dividends were paid, amounted to $829 million. What did Regis do with this money? Regis spent almost a billion dollars on acquisitions, it was building a Regis empire—beauty schools, Hair Club for Men (and Women), and Trade Secret, a high-end salon and product company. I'm surprised they didn't buy the rights to the musical *Hair*.

I know, in the context of trillion-dollar bailouts, a billion dollars doesn't sound like much, but it is a lot of money for a company with a $1 billion market capitalization. Just think of the magnitude of value destruction here. If management was only allowed to run its core business and all free cash flows just accumulated in the bank, and no acquisitions were made, the company would be sitting on a billion dollars of additional cash today. Regis wouldn't have had to issue shares during the crisis because it could not roll over its debt. With a billion dollars in the bank, its market capitalization would be nearly twice the current billion dollars. Just imagine what this company would be worth if it was run by a different kind of management.

I'll keep repeating this over and over: The value of any asset is the present value of its cash flows, but there is an implicit assumption that those cash flows are either returned to shareholders in the form of dividends or stock buybacks, or reinvested when return on capital exceeds its costs. Regis management did neither.

I always ask myself a question when I look at a company: What will management do with its cash flows? As we see from looking at Regis, the answer to this question is very important.

Recurrence of Revenues Beats Consistency of Earnings

Bernie Madoff's hedge fund returns never fluctuated; they went up 1 percent a month or so for almost two decades. Of course, as Madoff investors discovered, it is a lot easier to draw straight-line returns on paper than to produce them in real life. As we also keep discovering a few times every decade or so, ruler-like corporate earnings growth is often a result of accounting wizardry, not business proficiency.

To find truly predictable earnings, you will need to dig deeper, below the surface of the reported numbers, and look at the actual business to identify the qualities that make companies' earnings predictable.

Companies that have high recurring revenue components usually exhibit lower sales volatility and greater predictability of their earnings and cash flows, thus exhibiting less operational risk.

A high level of recurring revenues creates higher predictability and sustainability, and this reduces risk for investors. It also removes a lot of strain from growth, since a company with high recurring revenues has to put forth a lot less effort to grow revenues. Companies whose customers need to buy their products or services on a consistent basis usually exhibit less earnings volatility and thus less risk than companies whose customers don't.

Revenue predictability is complemented by product disposability. Let's contrast two very different companies: a home builder (MDC Holdings) and a medical instrument company (Becton Dickinson, maker of disposable needles and syringes). Home builders have absolutely no recurrence of revenues in their business. None! They buy land, build a house, sell the house, and move on to the next new house. Becton Dickinson, in contrast, has incredible recurring revenues—you use a needle and/or a syringe once and throw it away. Before you know it you need another.

Continuous demand for needles and syringes depletes the supply in the market. Home builders are quite the opposite. Once a house is built and purchased, it ultimately increases the future supply—new homes compete with existing homes. In other words, a home builder's past success competes with its future sales. To increase sales, a home builder has to sell as many homes as it did the previous year, plus some. Becton Dickinson doesn't compete with its past, since the needles and syringes it sold last year are already thrown away. The past may haunt home builders for a long time, since homes are a long-term asset. People who want to buy a home will have plenty of choices available from the houses that were built in preceding years, and looking at the rise of the construction industry over the past decade, there'll be a lot of those.

What does it all mean? Should you forever avoid investing in home builders? No, there have been ample opportunities to make money in home-building stocks, and there is an appropriate time to own them, though usually not right after a significant supply has flooded the market. Timing is extremely important when buying companies that produce highly durable products such as houses, capital equipment, and the like that have a very long useful life. These companies compete against external competitive threats and their own past sales. You should also be aware of the increased risk that comes with their earnings and for that matter the earnings of any company that doesn't have high recurring revenues. The risk of earnings volatility should be compensated by the strength of the company's balance sheet (which will be discussed next) and/or increased margin of safety (which I'll address in Chapter 8).

Debt Is Good, Except When It's Not

Often companies that could afford to use debt don't, and the ones that shouldn't, do. High return on capital and significant free cash flows usually lead investors to companies that underutilize debt.

Two industries that should not use debt but use it excessively are the U.S. auto manufacturers and airlines (most U.S. airlines, with the exception of Southwest and a few others). They have high fixed costs—planes and factories are expensive and, to a large degree, their expense is independent of the level of sales generated, a classic definition of operational leverage. They are highly unionized, and therefore it is difficult to lay off employees—their employees are a fixed cost as well. Their businesses are extremely sensitive to cyclical economic growth, since cars and air travel are mostly big-ticket discretionary items and the first to get cut by consumers and businesses when economic growth slows.

This combination of high operational and high financial leverages mixed with volatile sales is a recipe for disaster. Costs do not decline with sales, leading to significant losses.

To make things even worse, a significant portion of costs is driven by unpredictable commodity prices—fuel costs for airlines and raw materials for auto companies—adding another layer of risk to their cash flows.

Companies that have little debt have more room to make mistakes. Debt is good when it is judiciously used by a company with stable and predictable cash flows. However, a company that has volatile cash flows and a high degree of operational leverage should use debt with great caution.

I'd love to say that one's analysis of debt is completed just by looking at debt ratios, but it isn't. It is a start but by no means the end of the liability analysis.

Underfunded defined-benefit plans and operational leases are neatly tucked away off the balance sheet. But they should be carefully analyzed and put back on the balance sheet.

Accept No Substitutes

Sustainable competitive advantage, high-quality management, predictable earnings, significant free cash flows, strong balance sheet, and high return on capital are the wish list for a quality company. Some of these metrics, like sustainable competitive advantage and good management, should not be compromised on—period. However, some are interchangeable, and weakness in one could be offset by strength in another. For instance, strong balance sheet requirements could be eased if a company has predictable earnings and cash flows. Or lack of significant free cash flows could be overlooked if a very large portion of capital expenditures goes for growth. But I'd recommend making as few sacrifices on quality as possible. Remember that it is very hard to make up for losses in a sideways market.

Chapter Seven

Brought to You by the Letter "G" (for Growth)

**Growth and value investing are joined
at the hip.**

—*Warren Buffett*

THE STOCK MARKET IS NOT A GUY you'd want to take home to meet your parents. Though he is passionate, and he might even promise to love you to eternity, his love could turn into indifference or hate in a New York minute.

As investors we want to capitalize on the stock market's unstable temperament and thus buy out-of-favor, high-quality stocks that are trading at attractive valuations when others dump them. Though the stock market will often circle back to the stock a while later and start singing love songs again, it is hard to know when his heart will change; it could take some time.

The strategy of buying out-of-favor stocks comes with the risk that a supposedly temporary breakup will turn into a longer separation and the stock becomes dead money—staying undervalued and not going anywhere for a long time. This is where growth comes in handy. A company that is growing earnings and paying a dividend is compensating for the wait, substantially reducing the dead-money risk.

Usually when investors talk about growth they mean earnings growth. Myopically they ignore dividends—a mistake we won't make. The growth dimension encompasses both growth of profitability (expressed as earnings or cash-flow growth) and dividends (expressed as dividend yield). When a company pays a high dividend, you are getting paid to wait for the stock to come back to appropriate valuation. Growing earnings are compressing the valuation spring (the P/E) under the stock.

Let's see how this works: If you purchase a $15 stock that produces $1 of earnings per share (EPS) today, it is trading at 15 times earnings. If the company's earnings are growing 15 percent a year, its earnings will double in five years to $2 a share. If at that time the stock trades at a depressed 12 times earnings or $24 (12 × $2), you still have made a decent 10 percent a year return. If the stock paid a 5 percent dividend in the meantime, your total annual rate of return would have been an even juicier 15 percent. And once the love serenades are sung again, P/E will expand on top of higher earnings, rewarding your patience with even higher returns.

Even if you have slightly overpaid for the stock, the growth will heal this problem in time. Time is your best friend when a company's earnings are rising and dividends are constantly deposited in a brokerage account, but it turns into an enemy when that is not the case. It is important to know the sources of a company's profitability growth. The per-share profitability growth could be illustrated as a pyramid flipped upside down (see Exhibit 7.1), where revenue growth is at the wider top of the pyramid and net income, free cash flows, earnings per share, and free cash flow per share flow to the narrower bottom.

If costs are growing at a slower rate than revenues, net margin will expand and net income growth will outpace revenue growth. If in addition the company buys back stock, the number of shares will decline (net income will be divided by fewer shares)—earnings per share growth will outpace net income growth. And finally, if a company is able to manage its fixed and operating assets

Exhibit 7.1   The Sources of Profitability Growth Pyramid

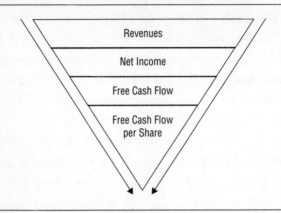

Source: Active Value Investing by Vitaliy Katsenelson (John Wiley & Sons, 2007, page 104). Reprinted with permission of John Wiley & Sons, Inc.

efficiently (achieve higher revenues without building new factories and/or holding the same inventory), free cash flow per-share growth will outpace growth of earnings per share. Shareholder value could be created on many levels of the company's operating pyramid, and therefore each level of the growth pyramid needs to be examined to see if it will be creating or destroying value.

Most things in life are finite, but each is finite to a different degree. Sources of growth are much the same. Although all face finality, it impacts them differently. Whereas some parts of the pyramid may have driven a company's growth in the past, these growth drivers may be approaching the last inning. You should revisit each growth driver regularly, with an expectation as to how much each driver can contribute to a company's future growth.

Revenue Growth

Growing revenues is the most natural way for a company to grow. There are several organic strategies for enabling a company to grow revenues.

Selling more products and services to existing and/or new customers. This is one of the most commonly followed strategies by corporate America and companies around the world.

Expanding to new markets, domestic or international. Apple expanded from being a computer company—mainly selling desktops and laptops—to an electronics company. In fact, in 2007 Apple dropped "Computer" from its name, signifying its encroachment into industries that lie outside of personal computers. Today it dominates digital music players, it is the largest seller of digital music, and its iPhones are quickly becoming the gold standard of smart phones. Many other companies have found a second life by going to growing international markets.

Raising prices. A tricky strategy, and its success depends on elasticity of demand (impact of higher prices on customers' willingness to buy the product). Raising prices is a finite strategy, as higher prices increase the attractiveness of the industry to new entrants. Depending on barriers to entry, these new competitors may attempt to capture market share by lowering prices. Or even worse, customers may just get frustrated with higher prices and switch to substitutes or competing products.

Lowering prices. Not the strategy that usually comes to mind, but it works if increase in demand offsets the decline in prices. Lower prices did wonders for the wireless industry, since they stimulated cell phone use and allowed wireless companies to spread fixed costs (the networks and customer service) among larger subscriber bases.

Of course there is also the growth-by-acquisition strategy, which is usually more expensive but is a way to grow business. Some companies have done a terrific job of growing by acquisition—CVS/Caremark, PepsiCo, L-3 Communications, and others. But as we saw with Regis, this strategy comes with its own set of risks.

Growth from Margin Improvements

Margin improvements may come from different sources, such as operating efficiency and economy of scale.

Above-average (high) profit margins in general are not sustainable in the long run—free markets are usually doing a good job of curing companies from above-average profit margins.

I often hear the argument: Over the last few decades companies have benefitted from technology. It made them more efficient and thus resulted in higher, above-average profit margins. However, as time goes on, technology that made one company more efficient becomes available to other industry participants. Those who adopt it will have a similar operating structure to the early adopter, while those who don't will be marginalized.

Profit margins are probably the most mean-reverting series in finance, and if profit margins do not mean-revert, then something has gone badly wrong with capitalism. If high profits do not attract competition, there is something wrong with the system and it is not functioning properly.
—Jeremy Grantham, GMO

As cost cutting becomes ubiquitous among the players, the cost structure among the competitors becomes similar. Competition is likely to drive prices and companies' margins lower, and customers will be the final benefactors of lowered operating costs as they receive the fruits of improved efficiency in the form of lower prices.

Therefore, it is difficult for a company to maintain competitive benefits from superior operating efficiency in the long run.

For example, Wal-Mart's rise in the retail industry was achieved through a very efficient inventory management and distribution system that passed cost savings to consumers and drove less efficient competitors out of business. Today, however, that same—or even better—technology is available off-the-shelf to retailers like Dollar Tree or Family Dollar, whose outlets are about the same size as a couple of Wal-Mart bathrooms. Oracle or SAP will gladly sell state-of-the-art distribution/inventory software systems to any outfit able to spell its name correctly on a check. Increased productivity didn't and won't bring permanently higher margins to corporate America. If profit margins didn't respond as they do, Wal-Mart's net margins would be 25 percent and not 3.5 percent, as they are today.

Cost cutting has a defined upper limit, since getting rid of *all* costs is a natural impossibility. A company may be successful at cost cutting for a while, but sooner or later it will hit its limit.

You want to make sure that cost cutting is not taking place at the expense of future growth. In the late 1990s, Becton Dickinson (a manufacturer of needles and syringes) was bringing to the market a safety needle-syringe system.

The company invested tens, if not hundreds, of millions of dollars developing the technology for this needle. A nurse drawing blood from an HIV patient, for instance, could not get infected using the new system. The Food and Drug Administration was about to require hospitals to use the new safety needle-syringe system. Analyzing the company at the time, I asked management about the competition and was told there was none.

The only meaningful potential competitor was U.S. Surgical, which was then purchased by Tyco. Tyco, a serial acquirer at the time, slashed U.S. Surgical's research and development (R&D) significantly, to immediately boost cash flows and please the short-term results-hungry Wall Street. Thus Becton Dickinson was coming to the market with a revolutionary syringe and U.S. Surgical had . . . well, nothing.

Economies of scale are a more sustainable source of margin expansion, but two things have to be present for economies of scale to materialize: sales growth and a high ratio of fixed to variable costs. In this case, as sales increase, costs don't rise as fast, leading to margin expansion. Similar to operating efficiency improvements, depending on the industry structure, at least some of the margin expansion will spill over to benefit customers in the form of lower prices (think Wal-Mart).

Stock Buyback

Stock buybacks at attractive valuations and nice, fat dividends create shareholder value. Absent a dividend or share buyback and assuming P/E doesn't change, to achieve 12 percent total return EPS needs to increase 12 percent. However, if the company paid a 3 percent dividend and bought back 2 percent of its shares, it would only have to grow earnings at 7 percent to achieve the same 12 percent total return. Usually, a company doesn't have to take as much risk to grow earnings 7 percent as it does for 12 percent earnings growth. Share buybacks are not a substitute for organic growth but are a bonus that is often underappreciated.

Stock buybacks can create shareholder value if the stock is purchased cheaply, but they often destroy value when management overpays for the stock. Stock buybacks raise two questions:

1. Is management a good investor?
2. Is the stock purchased in order to make the numbers (to meet or beat Wall Street's expectations of earnings per share)?

More often than not, company management isn't a good investor; it is blindsided by its love for the company. It spends an enormous amount of time to increase the company's profitability and to build a stronger franchise. This investment of time creates an attachment to the company, leading to a loss of objectivity. In the same way that parents lose objectivity as far as their children's abilities are concerned (e.g., I truly believe that everything my 4-year-old daughter Hannah draws is a masterpiece), management often overestimates the company's value and overpays when buying back stock.

An even worse reason that management is prone to overpay for company stock is that their compensation is often linked to EPS growth. And they will often do anything to stimulate that growth, even if it means destroying shareholder wealth through stock buybacks. Many American blue chips (Colgate, Wal-Mart, Sysco . . . the list is very long) were buying back stock in the late 1990s at ridiculous valuations because it was fashionable to do so and because they needed to show the market earnings growth.

If you are analyzing a company in your portfolio and come to the conclusion that the company should not buy back stock at today's valuation, ask yourself the question: "If I don't want the company to buy its stock at this price, is there a reason why I should continue to own it?"

Stock buybacks when the company stock is undervalued make sense. This is exactly what value investors do—buy undervalued assets. Adding debt to buy back stock is not as attractive as buying it from free (discretionary) cash flows, for two reasons:

1. Higher return comes with higher risk, possibly putting downward pressure on the company's P/E and thus offsetting benefits from a share buyback.
2. Leveraging the company's balance sheet has limitations (the company can take on only so much debt), whereas share buybacks from free cash flows over time are limited only by shares outstanding.

You should analyze stock buybacks on a case-by-case basis, asking these four questions:

1. Is the stock being purchased when it is undervalued?
2. What is management's motivation for the stock buyback?
3. Is the company leveraging its balance sheet to buy back stock?
4. Is there a better use for this cash?

Increased Efficiency

Improvements in working capital efficiency lead to higher free cash flows and thus make a company more valuable.

Dell has been shifting the burden of inventory to its suppliers for years. If suppliers want to do business with Dell, they have to deliver inventory to Dell in a matter of days, if not hours. As a result, Dell carries only several days of inventory—a crucial factor in an industry that faces constant price deflation.

The Past Has Passed

Just because a company was able to rely on a source of growth in the past doesn't mean it can count on it in the future. I strongly recommend that you not project past growth into the future with blind linearity.

Identifying sources of future earnings growth and examining each source individually should give you a deeper understanding of what makes a company tick, and it forces you to be more objective and forward-looking in your analysis. You should forecast the rate of growth for each engine separately at first, and only after that put them together. Being able to quantify the impact of each growth engine on the company's valuation will help you maintain a rational mind when things don't go as expected.

Finding companies that have several growth engines at the core of their growth reduces investment risk; if one growth engine fails or temporarily stalls, the other engines may still be driving the company's growth forward.

If you know the range of possible growth scenarios, you will be able to use the discounted cash flow model, discussed in depth in the next chapter, to determine the stock's value range.

What Dividends Really Tell You

Jan L. A. van de Snepscheut must have been talking about dividends and stock buybacks when he said, "In theory there is no difference between theory and practice. In practice there is." Though in theory there is no difference between dividends and stock buybacks, in practice there is. Dividend cuts send a negative signal to investors, in the extreme sending the stock into a tailspin and costing management their jobs, so management will sell their corporate jets and cancel their country club memberships before they dare cut the dividend. Even when earnings keep getting worse, companies often sacrifice their dividend payout ratio and maintain the dividend.

Share buybacks, however, are optional. Though a company may have authorization to buy back a certain amount of stock, the actual buyback execution is under management's control. Share buybacks are, in theory, as value-creative as dividends, but the absence of strict management accountability makes them unpredictable and thus less value-creative than dividends.

Usually, corporate management receives stock options that become more and more valuable as the stock price appreciates. This type of management incentive is poorly aligned with total return to the shareholder and so it is no wonder that management will tend to err on the side of buying back stock, rather than establishing a dividend.

Often a significant dividend creates a floor under the stock. As the price of a stock declines, its dividend yield increases, attracting more income-seeking investors and arguably reducing further downside price pressure.

Higher Dividend = Slower Growth?

In theory, companies that have a relatively high dividend payout should grow earnings at a slower rate than those that don't pay dividends. Intellectually this makes sense: Paying out more earnings leaves less to be reinvested in growing the business. In reality this only makes sense at the extreme. A great number of publicly traded companies have passed the stage where they can use all of their free cash flow to fuel further growth. These companies have excess cash flows that are available to pay higher dividends.

A study conducted by Cliff Asness and Robert Arnott, called "Surprise! Higher Dividends = Higher Earnings Growth," published in the *Financial Analysts Journal*

(January/February 2003) showed that companies that had a higher dividend payout actually grew earnings faster. In the summary of their findings, these authors write: "The historical evidence strongly suggests that expected future earnings growth is fastest when current payout ratios are high and slowest when payout ratios are low."

This study goes against theory, because theory doesn't factor in the destruction of capital by corporate management. (Regis, the hair salon company we discussed in the last chapter, is a poster child for lack of earnings growth due to low dividend payout. Regis squandered the cash it did not pay out.) A company that has high dividend payout operates in a different environment from the one that is swimming in shareholder cash, since rigid dividend payouts force management to maximize the value of every dollar retained. Higher dividend payout can instill discipline without hurting growth prospects.

Dividends and Sideways Markets

In *The Future for Investors*, Jeremy Siegel says that dividends serve as bear market protectors: "The greater number of shares accumulated through reinvestment of dividends cushions the decline in the value of the investor's portfolio." He goes further: "But extra shares do even more than cushion the decline when the market recovers. Those extra shares will greatly enhance future returns. So in addition to being a market protector, dividends turn into a 'return accelerator' once stock prices turn up. This is why dividend-paying stocks provide the highest return over stock market cycles." (Crown Business, 2005, page 318).

In addition to quantifiable financial benefits, a decent dividend instills confidence about the company's business. Earnings represent a myriad of accounting assumptions. Dividend checks are cut from cash flows, not earnings, so there is less of a chance that a company that pays a considerable dividend will engage in creative accounting wizardry.

During the twentieth century, average dividend yield was 4.3 percent. Current yield is less than half of that, floating around the lowest levels of the past 100 years. Dividends paid on an average stock or a broad market index (like the S&P 500) are unlikely to provide any salvation and will be of little help in protecting and accelerating returns in sideways markets. On the other hand, a portfolio of stocks with higher than average yields should achieve that objective.

As discussed in Chapter 2, the importance of dividends quadruples in sideways markets, where they historically represent over 90 percent of total return, versus only 19 percent of total return in bull markets.

Dividends Are Very Important, But . . .

Dividends are a part of the analytical equation but should never be mistaken for the whole equation. Although dividends are an extremely important contributor to portfolio returns in the sideways market, they should be secondary to other factors. Past dividend payments are not a guarantee of future dividend payments. During the Great Recession, investors who held on to bank stocks because of their high dividend yields learned this painful lesson. In other words, don't automatically buy a stock just because it pays a high dividend. This also applies to earnings growth; both are very important value creators in the sideways market. Neither should be approached in isolation (without consideration for Quality and Valuation dimensions), but both should be important components of your overall stock analysis.

Chapter Eight

Brought to You by the Letter "V" (for Valuation)

EVEN IF A CARPENTER FINDS THE HAMMER to be his favorite tool, he never comes to the job with just a hammer (at least not intentionally, not if he is sober). He brings his toolbox with a full set of tools in it.

It's the same with investing: You have many valuation tools at your disposal, and they all have advantages and drawbacks. However, by using them in concert with one another and by being aware of their strengths and weaknesses, you can make a more accurate valuation of any given company.

Beyond the Hammer

Relative valuation tools such as price-to-cash flow, price-to-earnings (P/E), price-to-sales, price-to-book, are good, quick, and easy shortcuts to analyze and screen stocks. Their ease of use have made them very popular among investors. For simplicity in this discussion I'll use P/E (the most popular of the bunch) to demonstrate the application of relative valuation tools and their use in the sideways markets.

Relative valuation analysis allows investors to see how a company's current P/E stacks up against competitors, industry averages, and the market. It also allows for historical comparisons. The P/E ratio is an important tool, if for only one reason—almost everybody uses it. The market has a view on stocks, and it expresses that view in the price it pays for a unit of earnings.

A value investor buying a stock wants to assess whether the stock is cheap or expensive. One way of doing it is to see at what P/E this company has changed hands in the past. If a company is currently trading at a P/E of 15 but it has never traded at a P/E higher than 12 in the past, it may not appear to be expensive on the surface but it is expensive relative to its past history. Market participants vote with their actions (buying and selling) and inactions on the amount they're willing to pay for one company's earnings versus its competitors'. Relative valuation analysis provides insight into how the market has voted on a company's valuation in the past.

A multitude of factors could have impacted past valuation, any of which may or may not repeat in the future. Some of these are:

- Historical P/Es may be reflecting a time period of high or low valuations that is unlikely to repeat in a foreseeable future.
- Past sales and earnings growth rates may be different from future ones.
- Significant changes may have taken place in the industry that changed the way investors look at the company.

Past valuation is not a guarantee of where the company will trade in the future; it is only one indication of what the future valuation may be. Now, let's look at discounted cash-flow (DCF) analysis—the commonsense model that Tevye used to estimate the value of Golde. It uses a multitude of assumptions from future sales to capital expenditures to profit margins. Once future cash flows are estimated, they are discounted (brought) back to the present at an appropriate discount rate (another major assumption) to find the estimated value of a stock. This result is then compared to an actual price. Many people would stop at this point, but this is just a start.

The DCF model output—the estimated intrinsic value of a company—is sensitive to assumptions that went into the model, and there are plenty of those. To expect that such a model will generate the exact stock value is unrealistic. At best, it shows direction of a stock's value.

The DCF model is a "vaguely right" model, and it should be used as such. As the final step and to find the likely range of a company's intrinsic value, one should change assumptions going into the model. Range of values doesn't have the sex appeal of a precise number, but keep in mind our goal is to be vaguely right rather than precisely wrong.

I often see sell-side analysts use the DCF model as a precise tool in research reports, saying something along the lines of: "XYZ stock at $10 appears to be undervalued by 7 percent, as our DCF model shows that it's worth $10.70." Often, all that analyst has to do is increase a discount rate by a fraction of a percentage point to see the estimated value of the stock drop and for that stock to become fully valued.

By trying different assumptions in your DCF model, you can find a set of them that lead to the current stock price. This should give you a good idea of what assumptions are priced into the stock by the market. You must then evaluate the stock's attractiveness based on achievability of these assumptions.

The DCF model is useful in extreme circumstances, in much the same way Tevye's analysis kept him out of the livestock auction on days one and two, when the Golde-like cows were selling at prices higher than the cash flows they'd be expected to generate over their lifetimes. DCF models would have also kept investors away from high-flying dotcoms and many other grossly overvalued stocks during the 1990s bubble.

On another hand, DCF analysis helps you gauge expectations built into a stock and gives you the confidence to buy an out of favor beaten-down stock with good potential for appreciation.

There is another hidden benefit of the DCF model—building the DCF model for a company should help you better understand its value creators and destroyers. This, in turn, will help focus your energy on those inputs that have larger impact on value creation: profit margins, sales growth, capital expenditures, accounts receivable, inventories, forecasted time period, and so on.

Look Both Ways before Crossing the Sideways Street

Though relative valuation tools are simple and intuitive, they have to be used with caution. This is especially true in sideways markets, since past valuations are unlikely to return in the not too distant future. Relative valuations benchmarked against those achieved in the past bull market or in early stages of a sideways market can thus lead to false buy signals.

Investors in the early 2000s may have justified their decision to buy Wal-Mart at 20 times earnings, assuming that it would once again trade at 45 times earnings, just as it did in 1999. This kind of thinking leads investors into a relative valuation trap. To avoid falling into this trap, investors in sideways markets should give priority to absolute valuation tools over relative ones.

In any market, margin of safety provides a cushion in case a company does not live up to investors' expectations and this is just a matter of time. However, when a company that trades at a discount to its intrinsic value disappoints by missing earnings estimates, or generating lower returns on capital, or achieving lower margins, its stock price is less likely to respond violently to such a disappointment than if the stock was fully valued.

A large margin of safety transforms a company into what amounts to a defamation-proof entity. In short, it can be compared to a person with such a terrible reputation that it is very difficult to say anything to defame or damage that person's reputation further. A company with a large margin of safety has already been defamed—it already has so much bad news priced into its stock that another round of bad news will likely go unnoticed. However, just a ray of unexpected sunshine may lift the stock up.

Margin of safety is a function of the following variables:

- Company's quality—its business and financial risks
- Investors' required rate of return for the stock
- Company's expected earnings growth rate
- Company's expected dividend yield

Should you require the same margin of safety for stocks of differing quality? Of course not. It is just a matter of time before a company stumbles. The strong ones will get up, regroup, and move forward. The weak ones may never get up; they may be liquidated, or may go bankrupt, leading to permanent loss of invested capital.

As we have discussed, stockholders are compensated in two ways: from the stock going up in price and from dividend payments. In the long run, stock appreciation can be explained by earnings growth and/or P/E expansion. If a stock is undervalued and likely to revert to the fairly valued level, P/E expansion is really just a margin of safety working in its "source of returns" role. Companies that have higher returns from dividends and earnings growth will require a lower margin of safety. This doesn't mean that you should not attempt to buy companies with large margins of safety that also pay high dividends and grow their earnings at fast rates but finding a portfolio full of such companies may prove to be difficult.

From Relativity to Absolutism

Now that we are equipped with various valuation tools, let's try to get some synergy from using them together.

I normally perform relative valuation analysis first, since it can tell you if a company has always traded at a premium or a discount to its peers. Relative valuation tools are important hints that are unlikely to bring you complete answers, at least not at first, but they will put you on the path to ask the right question: why? Why does a company (or industry) trade at a premium or a discount to its peers (or market)? The answer could be that it is due to differences in growth rates, or perception of management quality, or capital structure, or return on capital and so on.

Then I do DCF analysis, playing with different good, bad, and ugly scenarios. For example, I may estimate a stock's fair value at $50 to $70 using only DCF analysis but having previously performed relative valuation analysis on the stock, I should be able to narrow down that range.

Merging all valuation techniques covers all the valuation angles and provides clear insight into what the company's true worth is. Buying companies at the right price and with the right margin of safety is not enough to succeed in sideways market, but it is a good start on the road to success.

Even though you should try to look at the company from many angles, using as many models as possible, some models are more appropriate for analysis of some companies than others. For instance, companies that use their balance sheet to generate earnings (mainly financial companies) are valued on price-to-book, where "book" is the company's assets less its liabilities. Price-to-book is the more appropriate model for banks, because their assets and liabilities are marked to market values frequently. However, price-to-book analysis fails to capture true value of companies that have a lot of intellectual property (such as software or pharmaceutical companies).

In some instances break-up (or sum of parts) analysis is more appropriate. eBay lends itself perfectly to traditional DCF, relative-P/E models (relative to its past and relative to its peers), and sum of parts analysis. However, since eBay owns several separate businesses (eBay Marketplaces—online auction; Skype—a voice-over IP provider; PayPal—an online payment service) that are growing at different rates and have vastly different competitive advantages, then valuing each business segment separately provides significantly more insight into the value of the company as a whole. Valuing each business separately and then adding all the parts together will also help you to identify where to focus your efforts.

Skype is an exciting business, but it is only worth three billion dollars of which eBay owns 30 percent, while eBay itself has market capitalization of close to $30 billion dollars. Therefore, getting the exact valuation on Skype may not be as important as valuing eBay's other businesses. PayPal, on the other hand, is growing at 20 to 30 percent a year and contributes one-third of eBay's total sales; it has a significant competitive advantage and has leapt ahead of its competition. I'd use a higher P/E, lower discount rate, and probably a higher growth rate for PayPal than for eBay's Marketplaces business, which is facing tough competition from Amazon and slowing growth rate. In addition, since the PayPal business is in high-growth mode and its margins are constrained by new investments in the business, I'd also use the price-to-sales ratio to compare PayPal's valuation with more traditional payment processing competitors—Visa and MasterCard.

When valuing a business, don't forget its stash of cash. eBay has $5 billion of net cash (cash less debt) in the bank. After separately valuing eBay businesses using the various tools we have discussed, add up all the parts and net cash to arrive at a good estimate of eBay's real worth.

———————— ∿ ————————

Price is what you pay. Value is what you get.

—*Benjamin Graham*

A Word of Caution

How do we deal with P/E compression that is at play in sideways market? This is probably the hardest question we have to answer. I've spent a lot of time looking at the last, 1966–1982, sideways market. I've studied performance of stocks with different P/Es (high and low) and found the following:

- High-valuation stocks performed the worst in terms of P/E change due to market's P/E contraction.
- The lowest P/E stocks consistently outperformed the highest P/E stocks, in many cases by a margin of 2:1.
- They suffered lower P/E declines at the time when the overall market was going through P/E compression. They also achieved higher P/E expansion when market P/E's expanded. (Several massive cyclical bear and cyclical bull markets occurred during the 1966–1982 secular sideways market, see Exhibit 2.2.) Also, their lower P/E led to higher earnings yield (E/P) and thus resulted in higher dividend yield, which was a significant part of total return.

- For high P/E "growth" stocks (at least that is what high P/E implied), growth (including both earnings growth and dividends) did not offset the massive P/E erosion brought on by the sideways market.

Historically, sideways markets have not been friendly toward P/Es in general. If what we learned about the 1966–1982 sideways market is representative of other sideways markets, they are brutally toxic to high P/E or so-called growth stocks.

The easiest way to combat P/E erosion is to increase the required margin of safety for stocks you have in your portfolio. Demanding a higher margin of safety will make finding new stocks to buy harder, but that's just as it should be! Your goal is to assemble a portfolio of significantly above-average opportunity stocks. Remember, the road taken by *average* stocks in past sideways markets led to meager returns—you want to do much better than that.

I cannot stress enough that you should be very cautious about how much you pay for growth. As a sideways market persists, investors become more indifferent to growth and are willing to pay less and less for it. If you own some of those high P/E stocks, you want to be absolutely sure that their growth will sufficiently compensate for the P/E contraction that they are facing.

Chapter Nine

Add It Up

$Q + V + G$

IN THE PREVIOUS CHAPTERS WE REVIEWED each dimension of the Quality, Valuation, and Growth framework on an individual basis. In this chapter we'll take the framework to the next crucial step: We'll put these three dimensions together and explore their interactions with each other. Also we'll answer the question: "Should you compromise on any of the dimensions of the QVG framework when selecting stocks for your portfolio and if 'yes,' what dimensions?"

Sorry, that's two questions.

One Out of Three: Not Enough

You found this "great" company/stock that receives high scores in *only one* QVG dimension. Should you buy it?

Quality—Yea; Valuation and Growth—Nay

A company that has a high score on all or most of the factors that we discussed in the Quality chapter, but lacks meaningful earnings growth and/or dividend yield and is overvalued, is not a good investment no matter how high-quality that company is.

H.J. Heinz, for instance, was a great, high-quality company in the late 1990s. Although it had some debt, it also had stable, noncyclical cash flows that provided respectable interest coverage; its return on capital exceeded 20 percent; it had the ketchup market mostly to itself worldwide, as its brand was synonymous with ketchup—an indisputably high-quality company. However, it was lacking on the growth and valuation fronts. In 1998 it was trading at about 23 times trailing earnings—not a shocking number, at least not in relation to other stocks at the time. Considering that it already owned the ketchup market, its growth prospects were in the low single digits since and the stock was not cheap.

In 2010, after 12 years of miniscule earnings growth, the stock has not budged and it is at best fairly priced, trading at 15 times earnings. Meagerly dividend payments were the only return shareholders received for owning H.J. Heinz since 1998.

High quality may prevent a company from disappearing as a business, but its overvaluation is likely to turn the stock into a dreadful investment. In addition, subpar growth will not bring to this high-quality company much-needed salvation from overvaluation. The "religion stocks" that we will discuss in this chapter often have similar characteristics.

Valuation—Yea; Quality and Growth—Nay

A company that scores high valuation marks (it's cheap) but lacks growth or quality faces a different fate. Time is like a ticking bomb for this company. Those hoping for the value gap to close—for the stock to go up—may find themselves lucky, or not. Since this stock scores low marks on the growth front, earnings growth and dividends will not come to the rescue. Thus, akin to catching a falling knife, one may catch it by the handle—or by the blade.

General Motors (GM), for example, mostly traded at a P/E of 6 to 10 for more than 20 years, except for some short time periods when its earnings dropped, raising its P/E or turning it negative. On the surface GM was a statistically cheap stock. Unfortunately, GM, once an exemplar of U.S. ingenuity and success, was crippled by its unions, lost market share to more efficient, better-run Japanese competitors, and went bankrupt in 2009.

Growth—Yea: Quality and Valuation—Nay

Let's look at a low-quality, overvalued company with fast-growing earnings (and/or above-average dividends). It may appear that time is on the company's side, as growing earnings and dividends may lessen the valuation gap over time. Similar to the previous case, low quality may get the company before it has a chance of growing out of its overvaluation. Or, perhaps, the company will grow out of its quality and valuation problems, but that road is full of surprises and, similar to the previous scenario, comes with a lot of risk.

A lot of dot-com companies of the late 1990s fell into this category; they were growing their revenues at fast rates, their valuations were high, and their competitive advantages were difficult to uncover. We know the fate of those companies; many of them went bankrupt and very few survived.

Success is a lousy teacher. It seduces smart people into thinking they can't lose.

—*Bill Gates*

Two Out of Three: Better, But Is It Enough?

A company that receives high marks in at least two dimensions should have a disproportionately better risk/return profile than the company that scores high in only one dimension. There are three possible combinations where two dimensions are high and one is lagging.

Quality and Growth—Yea; Valuation—Nay

Many investors don't make the distinction between a great company and a great stock—an important cognitive error, perhaps one of the most common fallacies in investing. It is often easy to identify a great company. It easily meets the Quality and Growth tests: it has great brands, a bullet-proof balance sheet, and a high return on capital; it consistently has grown revenues and earnings and is expected to continue to do so. But a great company may or may not be a great stock.

A company scoring high Quality and Growth marks but lacking on the Valuation front has to overcompensate by having *very* high Quality and Growth marks. A combination of earnings growth and dividend payment has to be high enough to offset the impact of possible P/E compression and the lack of margin of safety.

It is important to realize that high Quality and Growth marks may not be high enough to offset a company's overvaluation. These marks may be an indication of a great company, but overvaluation may make this great company not a good stock! In other words, you may want to work for one of these companies, but you may not want to own the stock.*

There are plenty of companies that score high marks on quality and growth tests in any market environment. However, the number of companies passing the value test is often dependent on the overall market valuation at the time of the analysis.

There is a certain type of company that falls into the "religion stock" category. A basic property of religion is that the believer takes a leap of faith—believing without expecting proof. Since emotion is involved, it takes a while for a company to develop this type of religious following: Only a few high-quality, well-respected companies with long track records ever become worshipped by millions

---

*A side thought: It must be quite demoralizing to be an executive working for one of the companies that are stuck in sideways markets (Wal-Mart, J&J, Medtronic, etc.). Your stock was overvalued in the late 1990s and early 2000s—you had nothing to do with it; investors drove the valuations sky high. You've done what you were hired to do—grow company earnings and cash flows at very respectable rates (12 to 15 percent a year over a 10-year period, depending on the company). But all your hard work (earnings growth) was eaten away by P/E compression. I know it is very hard to invoke sympathy for executives of Fortune 500 companies today, but stock-price stagnation over significant periods of time must be reducing executives' drive to perform. Just a thought.

of unquestioning investors. When it happens, however, everybody recognizes these great companies, turning them into so-called religion stocks, the you-cannot-go-wrong-owning-this-company type of stocks, pushing their valuations to ridiculous levels.

To achieve the religion stock designation, a stock has to make a lot of shareholders happy for a long period of time, sufficient for them to perform the psychological leap of faith. Having high-quality brands readily identifiable with products or services that are widely used in everyday life is helpful but not necessary. The stories, which are often true, of relatives or friends buying a few hundred shares of the company and becoming millionaires have to percolate a while for a stock to become a religion. Little by little, the past success of the company turns into an absolute—and eternal—truth. Investors' belief becomes entrenched; past success paints a clear picture of the future, pointing the way to investor salvation.

Gradually, investors turn from cautious shareholders into loud cheerleaders. Management is praised as visionary. The stock becomes a one-decision stock—buy! This happened to the Nifty Fifty stocks of the mid-twentieth century and select technology stocks in the late 1990s. This euphoria is not created overnight; a lot of healthy pessimists have to be converted into believers before a stock becomes a religion—and a hefty P/E reflects that.

Coca-Cola in the late 1990s was a classic example of a religion stock. There were very few companies that had delivered such consistent performance for so long and had such a strong international brand name as Coca-Cola. It was hard not to admire the company. But admiration of Coca-Cola rose to irrational levels in the late 1990s, and it was saddled with a P/E that was pushing 50, much higher than the market's P/E. The company may not have had a lot of business risk, but by 1999 the high valuation was pricing in expectations that were impossible for this mature company to meet.

"The future ain't what it used to be"—Yogi Berra never lets us down. Old age and arthritis eventually catch up with religion stocks as well. No company can grow at a fast pace forever and growth eventually decelerates. Coca-Cola's famed consistent double-digit earnings growth failed its faithful believers and over the next dozen years it delivered half the growth rate of the preceding decades.

For Coke, the descent from its status as a religion stock resulted in a price drop from a high of $89 in 1998 to $55 in 2010. Even at $55, the stock was still not cheap, trading at 18 times 2009 earnings, despite expectations for earnings and sales growth in the mid-single digits.

Another religion stock was GE—a company that could do no wrong. However, once the religious, unconditional, in-GE-we-trust veil was lifted by the financial crisis and its stock collapsed, many found it to be just another complex, unanalyzable financial conglomerate that was suffering from addiction to the commercial paper market. There is nothing new I can say about GE except that it represents what is wrong with religion stocks—they are bought, and in many cases held, on faith. Few attempted to value GE beyond looking at reported ruler-like earnings that management manipulated by changing pension plan assumptions and shifting reserves through opaque GE Finance. GE (similar to many other very large financial companies) is like a hot dog—you don't really know what goes into it.

It takes a while for the religion premium to be totally deflated because faith is a strong emotion. A lot of frustration with subpar performance has to come to the surface. Disappointment chips away at faith one day at a time.

Religion stocks are not safe stocks. Irrational faith and false perception of safety come at a large cost—the hidden risk of reduction in the religion premium (i.e., high valuation). The risk is hidden, because it never came to the surface in the past. Religion stocks, almost by definition, have had an incredibly consistent track record; risk was rarely observed. However, this hidden risk is unique, because it is not a question of *if* it will show up but *when* it will show up. It is hard to predict how far the premium will inflate before it deflates—but it will deflate eventually. When it does, the damage to the portfolio can be tremendous. In addition, religion stocks generally have a disproportionate weight in portfolios because they are never sold—exposing the trying-to-be-cautious investor to even greater risks.

Religion stocks often pass the quality test with flying colors, as past success was driven by a strong sustainable competitive advantage. What is the greatest danger with religion stocks? It is that faith, which was built on past performance, leads investors to believe that high growth is still ahead for the company and often this is not the case. The next greatest danger of religion stocks is that, without earnings and cash-flow growth, there is little to cushion their stock price from falling when P/Es contract. A stock's behavior when its P/E premium deflates depends on many factors, but stock market performance and company earnings growth are at the top of the list.

Sideways markets are agnostic deflators of the religion premium, turning religion stocks into a subpar class of investments. You need to maintain an agnostic view of religion stocks, since the comfort and false sense of certainty that these stocks bring to the portfolio come at a huge cost—prolonged underperformance.

Quality and Valuation—Yea; Growth—Nay

It happens quite often: You find a great company that has a great brand, strong competitive advantages, a solid balance sheet, nice return on capital, and more. It has an attractive valuation, at least on the surface. It dominates the market where it competes, but its market is not growing fast and it has taken the entire market share that was there for the taking—it is a slow-growth company.

What should you do? Avoid slower-growth companies altogether? Maybe not, but you can do these two things.

First, require an increased margin of safety. Let's say you have two stocks: A is growing earnings at 6 percent a year and pays a 4 percent dividend, and B has 0 percent growth and doesn't pay a dividend. Stock A is paying you to hold it; the dividend enriches your brokerage account by 4 percent a year and growing earnings increase the value of the stock by 6 percent a year (its fair value should increase 6 percent, even if the price doesn't reflect that at any given moment). Time is on your side if you own stock A. Stock B is a very different story.

Its value is static as earnings are not growing and your brokerage account is lonely—no dividend checks are coming in.

If your analysis leads you to believe that each stock is worth $100, you may want to require a 30 percent discount to fair value for stock A and thus be willing to purchase it for $70. With stock B, however, you should require a higher margin of safety. Instead of looking for a 30 percent discount, as you did with stock A, you should be asking for a higher number. How much? It will depend on how long you think you'll have to wait for the market to price the stock appropriately. The purchase price you set for stock B should certainly be below $70 that you chose for stock A—the longer you expect to wait, the higher the discount should be.

My second suggestion is to look for a catalyst—an event that would close the margin of safety gap within a specific time frame. A catalyst is an event that would bring investor interest back to the undervalued stock, driving the stock to its fair value. It could take many different forms, such as a corporate restructuring or the sale of underperforming or noncore assets, which unlocks shareholder value. A new management team may turn the company's operations around, as well. The company could also be bought by another or taken private through a leveraged buyout by current management.

Here are two catalyst questions to ask:

1. How certain are you that the catalyst will occur?
2. Will the catalyst attract enough investor interest to drive the price of the stock to fair value?

Valuation and Growth—Yea: Quality—Nay

This is the most dangerous combination of all: A company is growing earnings at a fairly fast rate and/or paying a dividend; it is attractively priced (at least relative to the growth rate) but has a quality flaw. Its competitive advantage may be thin, it may be overleveraged, its return on capital may be below the cost of capital, or revenues may not be recurring.

It is difficult to generalize about this scenario, as quality issues are diverse in nature. Looking for salvation in a higher growth rate or an increased margin of safety may or may not be enough. For instance, if the incremental return on capital is below the company's incremental cost of capital, high growth is only going to hurt the company, destroying shareholder value in the process.

The exception here is when a company's return on capital suffers from lack of scale. Growth could save the company by sufficiently increasing scale (spreading higher revenues over the same fixed costs) and improving return on capital.

A heavily leveraged company cannot afford to make even a small mistake, since the consequences could be dire, and even a huge margin of safety may not provide a safe haven if disaster strikes. Investors should focus on severity and diversity of the quality issues. One quality flaw should be compensated by the strength of another quality factor. For instance, a company with volatile or unpredictable revenues should have a very strong balance sheet.

If you were to look at most fashion retailers, especially the ones that sell stuff to teenagers—the likes of American Eagle Outfitters or Abercrombie & Fitch—these retailers carry very little debt and have huge cash balances. There is a significant fashion risk in what they sell. Worn-looking jeans with giant holes could become uncool in a New York minute—teenagers are not known for their stable and predictable tastes. Sales could take a dive very fast, turning a profitable company into a money-losing one. In this case the fad quality flaw is more than offset by strong balance sheets.

Little can help a company that has no competitive advantage. A strong balance sheet may prolong its life expectancy, but it will not save the company from its less-than-happy fate. Even if a company has a high return on capital, that is likely to be a temporary phenomenon, if a competitive moat is not there to protect the return on capital from competitors encroaching on that company's turf.

Compromise? Not!

Do not compromise on more than one dimension, since that introduces too much risk and often leads to subpar returns. Each of the Quality, Valuation, and Growth dimensions is an important source of value creation. Valuation and Growth, as Warren Buffett put it, "are joined at the hip," being the source of returns, while Quality makes sure that the company will still be around to collect the fruits of its labor.

Chapter Ten

Nip/Tuck

~

*Think Long-Term, Act Short-Term
in a Sideways Market*

LONG-TERM INVESTING IS AN ATTITUDE, an approach to analysis. By that, I mean focusing the thought processes on deciding whether to make an investment in the company (the business) at the right price, not on trying to make a speculative trade in the stock.

This investment philosophy, the way you approach company analyses, doesn't need to change in the sideways market. But the buy-and-sell processes, the execution of one's investment philosophy, do require some tweaking.

Buy-and-hold is really just a code name for a "buy and forget to sell" strategy. A stock likely went through a fairly rigorous buy process but "hold" is just camouflage for the absence of a tangible sell process, unless you call "I'll own it till death do us part" a sell process. "Buy and forget to sell" works great in a prolonged bull market. P/Es keep expanding from much below to much above average. However, as we've seen in previous chapters, the complete opposite to bull market behavior takes place during the sideways market.

In the sideways market you should employ an active buy-and-sell strategy: buying stocks when they are undervalued and selling them when they are about to be fully valued, as opposed to waiting until they become overvalued.

Meet Your New Best Friend—Volatility

A sideways market is at least not boring. We may end up where we started, but what a ride it was. Sideways markets are very volatile and the ride may be exciting, but the returns are not.

You need to befriend volatility; it should be respected and used to your advantage. I am not suggesting that you try to time the market by going to cash at the top and becoming fully invested (mortgaging the house, pawning your favorite cat) at the bottom. Although tops and bottoms are obvious when looking at historical charts, they are not usually evident in real time.

A market timer's buy and sell decisions are made based on predicting the short-term direction of stock prices, interest rates, or the condition of the economy. It is hard if not impossible to create a successful market-timing process. Aside from the fact that it demands that you be correct twice—when you buy and when you sell—emotions are in the driver's seat of the market, especially at the tops and bottoms. Even if you get the economic event right and Lady Luck kisses you on the cheek and you nail its timing, the market may just spit in your direction and chose to ignore it till a later date. In summer of 2007, for example, the housing bubble finally burst, bringing the toxic waste (sub-prime) loans to the surface. Credit markets froze . . . and you'd think the stock market would decline? No, the Dow went on to an all-time high, hitting 14,000 and ignoring the problems for months.

In fact, the worst thing that can happen to you is being right once about a change in market direction. You'll think that you figured it out, although you really didn't. Randomness was just playing a trick on you, and you will lose (or not make) money if you fall for it.

Time Stocks, Not the Market

_____ ∾ _____

**I used to be bullish, then I was bearish.
Now I'm brokish!**

—*Milton Berle*

_____

Instead of trying to time the market, my answer to volatility is to time individual stock valuations through a strict buy-and-sell process. If you don't like the word *timing*, call it *pricing*—you need to price individual stocks. You buy them when they are undervalued and sell them when they become about fully valued.

To time stocks, first break stock analysis into the three dimensions of Quality, Valuation, and Growth, and then combine the analyses. To avoid falling into the alluring "good company/bad stock" trap, or even worse, the "religion stock" emotional trap, make company analysis (quality and growth) and stock analysis (valuation) two separate steps and then ask two separate questions:

1. Is XYZ a good company?
2. Is XYZ a good stock (investment)?

To take this a step further, if both (good company and good stock) conclusions lead to "yes," the stock is bought.

If the good-company test is failed, move on to the next stock—there are a lot more stocks where that one came from! However, for the companies that pass the good-company test but fail the good-stock test, create a wish list or "Companies I Would Love to Own at the Right Price" list.

For every company you find worthy of owning (high quality and growth marks), set the optimal price or valuation level at which it transforms into a good stock. First determine the fair value using a combination of relative and absolute valuation tools. Then settle on the required margin of safety (the discount to the fair value) that will lead to the buy P/E. And finally (the hardest part), sit and patiently wait for the stock to come down to the predetermined target valuation level and/or price.

Using a valuation target such as P/E (or price to cash flows, price to book, and so on) has an advantage versus a price target. As time passes and earnings grow, the specific price target becomes less meaningful, since it was created at a time when earnings power was lower (or higher). Thus, even as the price goes up, if earnings power increases at a faster pace, the stock could still be an attractive purchase.

A benefit of creating the wish list is that the valuable time spent on analysis doesn't go to waste, even if no stock is purchased immediately. The opportunity will often present itself later to buy a good company on attractive terms, at a good price. Assembling this wish list will liberate you from emotional attachment to good companies. It will align your emotions with the truth that investing is not about feeling good about owning good companies at *any* price but rather is about making money while taking a reasonable amount of risk.

Doing Nothing Is Really Something

The number-one objective should be not to lose money, and thus you should try to avoid making marginal decisions: Don't buy stocks that have not scored appropriate marks on all three dimensions of the Quality, Valuation, and Growth framework.

Blaise Pascal said, "All man's miseries derive from not being able to sit quietly in a room alone." You need to be able to sit on your hands and do nothing unless or until a great investment opportunity presents itself. That is a difficult thing to do, especially when stocks are constantly moving up and down, news is being released in torrents, earnings are being reported, and so much action is happening.

Not participating in hysteria is what separated Tevye from other farmers, the ones who spent their money on day one of the livestock auction and lost much of it on day three. Tevye had the mental fortitude to "sit on his hands" on days one and two of the auction; he had no tangible results to show, since no cow was purchased. In fact on those days, when he came home to his second wife, Haffka (he would not name a cow after her), and told her he hadn't bought a cow, she inquired accusingly, "What *did* you do then?" Tevye patiently explained, "I was looking for my Golde but did not find her."

Tevye had a clear idea of what qualities his Golde would have and what price he would pay for her. During the first two days of auction, despite the euphoria, a few cows appeared cheap, at least on the surface. But Tevye patiently let other farmers bid on them because they lacked the qualities he was looking for. He knew that while the weather stayed warm those cows would do okay, producing as much milk as his Golde, but God forbid the weather should turn cold—these cows would grow weak, and then suddenly what appeared to be a "cheap" cow will be not be cheap anymore.

So Tevye's inaction on days one and two was a well-informed, determined action in itself.

In 1998, at Berkshire Hathaway's annual meeting, Warren Buffett said, "We don't get paid for activity, just for being right. As to how long we'll wait, we'll wait indefinitely." Buffett plays bridge in his "do nothing" time, while his right-hand man Charlie Munger works on his mental models by reading books on various intellectually stimulating subjects.

In a raging bull market cash is your biggest enemy, because that boat doesn't rise with the tide of a rising market. As we discussed in Chapter 3, the lost opportunity cost of being in bonds or cash is high during bull markets, but in sideways markets when fixed-income instruments are a fair contender for your capital in the absence of attractive stocks, cash is not a bad friend to have.

If you are a market timer, your cash balance is a function of what you think the market is about to do. However, the stock timer's cash balance is a by-product of investment opportunities that appear in the market. If you can't find good stocks that meet your QVG criteria, cash or short-term bonds are good alternatives until a new opportunity presents itself. You should not buy stocks for the sake of being fully invested.

I have no desire to attempt to forecast short-term and long-term interest rates or the yields of money-market funds, but no matter what these instruments' yields are, as long as they are not negative, they are preferred to a marginal investment. Unless you find stocks offering superb returns that are commensurate with the level of risk taken, your money should be parked in cash.

Be Ready to Strike When the Time Comes

Professional investment managers don't have the luxury of playing bridge or reading books on subjects unrelated to investing (the history of civilization, perhaps, or the last ice age), at least not on the company's dime. Even if you are investing at home you'll face a similar problem—spouses (like employers) just don't seem to understand that by doing nothing we are following in the footsteps of great investors! "Do nothing" time should be used to increase one's areas of expertise. You should prepare for the battle by researching companies that score high quality and growth marks and by finding companies that should be put on your wish list. Then, monitor the situation and when the time comes and a company on your wish list hits the target buy valuation, strike without hesitation.

Chapter Eleven

The Born-Again Value Investor

~

The Importance of Going against the Grain in a Sideways Market

WHAT DOES IT REALLY MEAN, being contrarian? Doing the opposite of what everybody else is doing, all the time? What if you agree with what everybody else is doing? Should you disagree for the sake of being contrarian?

Hardly. Being contrarian means being able to think and act independently of the crowd and not being swayed by crowd thinking. It means staying on your own track, independent of the direction the crowd is taking, whether that requires going against or with the crowd. It means not accepting the market's wisdom unconditionally but rather attempting to develop an opinion of your own.

~

When people agree with me I always feel that I must be wrong.

—*Oscar Wilde*

Being a contrarian or an independent thinker is vital for success in a sideways market. This is a time when you must exercise disciplined buy and sell processes for an extended period. A contrarian state of mind is needed when selling into the rallies as stocks become fully valued, since this is usually a time of great excitement about stocks in general and the crowd is buying. Conversely, buying into sell-offs, when conventional wisdom says the market is not where you want to be—but the stocks on the watch list start hitting their buy valuations—requires an unemotional and often courageous contrarian mindset.

We feel more comfortable and more certain about the future when the investment crowd (especially the one in our immediate surroundings) is on our side of the market fence. Since we want to feel good about our decisions, doing what the crowd does provides the comfort that we constantly seek. Not following the crowd or, even worse, making decisions that are contrary to the crowd's may try our convictions and bring on self-doubt.

It was easy to follow the crowd in the late 1990s. For instance, that crowd loved Sun Microsystems to death; it reached a high of $64 in 2000, but then settled into the single digits by early 2002 and was acquired by Oracle for $9.50 per share in 2009. Following is an excerpt from a 2003 *BusinessWeek* interview with Scott McNealy, the CEO and founder of Sun Microsystems, in which he responds to a question about the crowd's thinking when it bid up Sun's stock to $64:

> Two years ago we were selling at 10 times revenues when we were at $64. At 10 times revenues, to give you a 10-year payback, I have to pay you 100 percent of revenues for 10 straight years in dividends. That assumes I can get that by my shareholders. That assumes I have zero cost of goods sold, which is very hard for a computer company. That assumes zero expenses, which is really hard with 39,000 employees. That assumes I pay no taxes, which is very hard. And that assumes you pay no taxes on your dividends, which is kind of illegal. And that assumes with zero R&D for the next 10 years, I can maintain the current revenue run rate. Now, having done that, would any of you like to buy my stock at $64?

There are times when the investing crowd behaves in irrational ways, and those are times when being an independent thinker is crucial, because following the crowd, although it provides emotional comfort, often comes with a cost associated with it—financial losses. This chapter outlines several ways to ensure that you're always thinking for yourself.

Plug Your Ears

In *The Odyssey*, the Sirens lured ships with their sweet songs to their island and then killed the sailors. As his ship was about to pass the Sirens' island, Odysseus, aware of the Sirens' power and his own inability to resist the sweetness of their songs, ordered his sailors to put wax in their ears and tie him to the mast (note he doesn't put wax in his own ears). As the ship passes the island, Odysseus endures the agony of the Sirens' ravishing songs and orders his sailors to change course toward the Sirens' island; but of course the sailors don't hear him (with their ears plugged with wax) and they stay on course.*

As the ship passes away from the island and the Sirens' singing fades, the sailors untie Odysseus and, unlike other Greek stories, this one doesn't end in tragedy.

---

*Nassim Taleb used the Odysseus story to illustrate a similar point in *Fooled by Randomness*.

Our modern adventurer, Mr. Investor, is constantly subjected to the siren songs of the stock market—sweet noise that is constantly emitted and amplified by the media. Unlike Odysseus, who intentionally brought upon himself the pain of wanting something he could not and should not have had and was willing to pay the price for the pleasure of hearing the Sirens' songs, Mr. Investor is involuntarily and constantly exposed to the toxicity of market noise, which damages his state of mind and turns him from an investor into a trader, while affording him little positive utility in return.

Investor morphed into trader would not be a bad thing (some of my good friends are traders), if investors were good at trading. Unfortunately, most are not. Rarely do a successful investor and a successful trader reside in the same skin. The investor's toolbox only comes with buy-low, sell-high (or buy-cheap, sell-dear) tools and a state of mind that usually fails in the domain of trading. For a trader, the concept of buying at a discount to intrinsic value is held in low regard and a buy-high, sell-higher mentality is prevalent in this Wall Street version of musical chairs.

Stock market volatility, and the poisonous noise that it brings, warp and compress Mr. Investor's time horizon, unleashing the demons of greed and fear and turning what used to be a rational buy-low, sell-high investor into a buy-high, sell-low emotional wreck. The investor's system of values—the rational process—is replaced by the one that the media sirens choose to promote at that moment.

Our sanity and the investment process should be protected, however, unlike Odysseus we should not tie ourselves to the mast and subject ourselves to the torture of media-amplified market noise, but rather we should plug our ears.

Though being aware of the impact that noise has on the investor's psyche is a start, it is not quite enough. The sheer volume and velocity of noise generated by the market and amplified by media breaks down and fatally clogs our noise-filtering mechanism. We should proactively and methodically create a protective environment where we limit (or block outright) the majority of outside noise that comes through, and only then should we start filtering.

Let's try to establish a rough baseline for a noise-free environment. Take yourself back to the 1960s and to a place far removed from Wall Street—it could be Omaha, or Denver (I personally like this one), or Jackson Hole, or any other hole, as long as the post office is able to deliver the newspapers and annual reports with their usual efficiency.

You are, as noted value investor Mohnish Pabrai puts it, a gentleman of leisure. *You* decide what is important for you and you consume information on your own terms, browsing newspapers and annual reports, studying industries and valuing businesses, reading investment books, and taking a nap, if you feel it makes you a better investor.

In the 1960s, discussions of the stock market on TV generated only slightly more excitement than watching a spelling bee. The stock market was not yet a national pastime, thus the media spent little or no time explaining why investors, at any given hour, collectively chose to price the Dow higher or lower. Of course, even in the 1960s, investors who greatly desired it could gain exposure to the daily stock market noise, but they had to make a very proactive and laborious effort to achieve that.

Now that we have established a baseline for the rational investor, the leisurely gentleman of the 1960s, let's fast-forward to today, where we find that progress, which at first sneaked in little by little, has now flooded in through the invention of personal computers, spreadsheets, the Internet and e-mail, BlackBerries and iPads.

I am not about to start advocating sending telegrams instead of e-mails or using an abacus instead of a spreadsheet and a calculator, but the state of mind of the leisurely investor needs to be protected, and thus "progress" should not be allowed into our lives unchecked.

The environment is everything that isn't me.

—*Albert Einstein*

How Often Should You Look at Your Stocks?

Let's start with something that appears to be very harmless: stock quotes. Checking stock prices on the Internet undoubtedly beats digging through stock tables in newspapers, but the ease and instant availability of stock quotes (or even worse, streaming quotes) glues us to the computer screen.

Ironically, long-term investors suddenly and inadvertently start judging the success and failure of their portfolios (that were set up with years in mind) on second-by-second ticks. Despite the ease of access, checking prices only a few times a day is sufficient—the fewer times you do it the more rational you'll remain.

Focus on a stock in the context of the total portfolio and focus more on whether the company QVG dimensions are still on track, rather than on daily or weekly share prices.

Media Are There to Drive You Insane

Over the years, serious business news that lacked sensationalism and thus high ratings was replaced by a new genre: business entertainment (of course, investors did not get that memo). Business entertainment found a way to fill the human need to have an explanation for everything, even random, unexplainable things. On-screen, an army of experts now guides us, by sound bites, through every tick of the stock move, telling us exactly why stocks declined in the morning, traded in a tight range during lunch, went up, then declined, and finished at the same level where they started.

Most information on a business entertainment channel has as much benefit for a value investor as a minute-by-minute weather report has for a traveler who is not planning to travel for another year. Business entertainment is a massive generator of noise, and every expert possesses the confidence of a Greek god, issuing proclamations as to what the stock market will do tomorrow, next week, next month, and next year. When a careless interviewer asks a question for which the expert does not have an answer, you'll still get an answer, for to pipe up and say "I don't know" will mean the expert will have his expert's hat taken away, and he won't be invited again because business entertainment is all about omniscience.

In reality, the stock market's short-term, intraday (or even day-to-day) movements are random, not much different from a ball traveling on a roulette table in Las Vegas. Short-term fluctuations are driven by millions of variables, which are impossible to predict—although that doesn't stop the business entertainment channel from conjuring up explanations. Within the same hour you may hear "Traders shrugged off the bad employment report as stocks moved higher" and "The market declined due to the unfavorable employment report."

I imagine most people would find it absurd if Bellagio had a round-the-clock televised program where well-dressed experts debated and explained why the ball on the roulette table landed on red and made predictions as to where the ball would land next. However, this is what is taking place on business TV all day long.

I don't want to overdramatize the noise generation of the business entertainment channels; not everything they produce is noise, but the ratio of substance (content of value) to noise is relatively small, and to get the substance one needs to consume and get poisoned by a lot of noise.

Knowledge in investing is cumulative—what we learned from analyzing one company or industry helps us with analysis in the future. However, the noise we accumulate from business entertainment just increases the noise level. It does not add to our store of knowledge.

I used to try to control the noise blaring from the TV box by keeping the business entertainment channel on indefinite mute (as most people I know do). However, TV executives figured us out and now the business enter-tainment channel uses flashy graphics and "breaking news" banners (that flash several times each hour) to attract occasional glances from muters like me.

My solution: I keep the TV off completely during the day. Instead, I watch the boring business shows, usually on PBS *(Charlie Rose* and *Wealth Track)*, where hosts and guests can have an intelligent conversation about meaningful topics, employing complete sentences (no sound bites there). Taking my traveler analogy further, at least on the boring business channel I learn something about the destination to which I am headed.

This brings me to a very important point: we need a process to protect our investment process; our sanity needs to be actively guarded.

Single-Task

I was six or seven years old. I was observing my maternal grandfather Berl watch TV and read the newspaper at the same time. Curious, I asked him how he could do both at once. He said, "It's called multitasking." He continued, "Oh, I am a dilettante at this, but Julius Caesar was the master of multitasking; he could watch TV, listen to the radio, read a newspaper, talk on the phone, and iron his pants, all at the same time."

It took me a long time to learn lessons from this off-the-cuff comment. First, my grandfather was not multitasking. He was not really watching TV, he was reading a newspaper. The TV was for my grandma; he just liked being in the same room with her. Second, 2000 years ago, men were not wearing pants, they were in robes, at best; so Mr. Caesar did not have to worry about ironing his pants. Oh yes, telephone, radio, and TV were not around back then either. Third, and unfortunately it took me 30 years to figure this one out, I am not Julius Caesar. In fact, I have some serious doubts whether Mr. Caesar would be a master of multitasking in today's world, which is even more technologically complex than the one in my grandfather's living room 30 years ago. This new world has been supersized by personal computers, the Internet, e-mail on multiple devices, texting, instant messaging, YouTube clips, and anything and everything that starts with "i."

Stanford University conducted an extensive study on multitasking, and they discovered something we should have known for a long time: We are horrible at it. They found that while we are multitasking we have a hard time ignoring irrelevant information, and we become too sensitive to new information. Let's think about the importance of this finding. If you are sweeping streets or bagging groceries, where analyzing, processing, and responding to new information is not at the core of successfully completing the task, then multitasking is not dangerous.

However, investing is a mental exercise at the heart of which lies our ability to rationally analyze, process, and respond to new information. To maintain a rational state of mind we should single-task.

There is another benefit of single-tasking. I vividly remember the four most productive hours I spent last year. I flew with my wife from Denver to Miami; I was to give a speech. We did not preregister, the plane was fully booked, and my wife and I were sitting a dozen rows apart. For the duration of the flight I did not have access to e-mail, and people next to me were reading books and not trying to strike up conversations. I politely put my headphones on and typed until my laptop's battery gave out. I wrote the entire speech, all 10 pages of it. I did zero multitasking on the plane.

This was a great lesson for me. Of course, to be more productive I could spend all my days in the air and rack up frequent flier miles, but I devised a more practical way to recreate an in-flight environment on a daily basis. For a good part of the day, I turn off my phones (that includes my cell phone), and shut off my laptop's Wi-Fi function, which kills the Internet connection and everything Internet-related: instant messenger, Skype, the browser, and e-mail. I turn on light classical music and start working.

––––––––––––––––––– ～ –––––––––––––––––––

Few people think more than two or three times a year; I have made an international reputation for myself by thinking once or twice a week.

—*George Bernard Shaw*

––

Write, write, write! We all think and learn differently; what works for me may or may not work for you. But I'll share with you another trick that I find very beneficial to maintaining a rational state of mind: I write. I find it a great tool to combat the sirens of the market. I *think* while writing. Some people can think in their office for hours while staring at the ceiling. If you are one of them, then ignore my advice; but if you are not, you may discover that writing is an active thinking process. I find that it is a great organizer of thought. My mind is like a Caesar salad; writing encourages me to look through the mound of lettuce and take out the croutons—the thoughts—and then put them in order.

Other Sound Contrarian Advice

The following advice is actually sound in any market, not just a sideways one, so it's always helpful to keep in mind.

You Don't Have to Own It. It is the stock that is on everybody's lips. It is hot. It is a "must own," or so you've been told. The usual comparisons are being thrown around—this one is the next Starbucks or Microsoft. But for every Microsoft and Starbucks there are hundreds of companies that have sunk into oblivion. We remember only the companies that succeeded, since they're still around to remind us of that; we don't remember the ones that failed—the Ataries of the world. When everybody is talking about a hot stock, it looks expensive to a value investor. It has no margin of safety to speak of; only hoped-for return is priced into the stock but very little risk.

Know What You Don't Know. Tevye understood certain areas of farming better than others. For instance, Tevye did not set out to buy a pig, for good reason. You may think the reason was his Rabbi's and the community's disapproval of a Jewish farmer raising an un-kosher animal. Though that could have been a part of Tevye's decision, there was a more pragmatic explanation: pigs do not give milk (or at least not milk that humans are willing to pay for and drink), and Tevye was a milkman.

He did not have a good feel for revenues that pigs would bring, and the risks were unclear to him. Does pork compete with the other white meat, chicken? Is there a mad pig disease? Pigs were outside of his core competence and so he stuck with cows. It is important to own stocks you can value, of companies you can understand. They have to be analyzable but not just analyzable: they must be understandable to *you*.

No Short-Term Pain, No Gain. Somewhere along the way of explosive growth in the mutual fund industry, our innate desire for short-term gratification altered the nucleus of the investment business, turning it into a marketing one. This mindset puts a premium on keeping up with the (Dow) Joneses and topping comparable indexes every quarter. That is not what investing is about; it is about reaching your long-term financial goals while taking the least amount of risk. The shortsightedness of investors creates an embedded incentive for market participants that control an enormous amount of capital (Wall Street) to favor stocks that are expected to do well in the shorter run. They will sell (or avoid) stocks with an ambiguous immediate future, even though these stocks may have a great risk/reward profile in the long run, which of course always lies past the short run. Therefore, if you can stomach the short run and have a longer time horizon than several calendar quarters, as any sensible investor should, an opportunity is created: time arbitrage (or I also like to call it, short-term pain arbitrage).

Own Your Work and Create a Paper Trail. To keep a sane head, independent of the direction in which the crowd is marching, write down your basis for every investment, identifying value creators and destroyers and your expectations for them. Similar to recording the sell valuation target for a stock at the time of purchase, an investment thesis committed to paper at that time represents the unemotional, clear-thinking, and rational you. Such paper trail will provide you peace of mind. No matter how volatile markets become, how persuasive the emotive crowd's behavior, or how high the media turn up the volume, you will have a lucid strategy for rational decision making.

Say Hola, Bon Jour, Guten Tag, Buon Giorno. Simply stated, stocks should compete against each other for a place in your portfolio. The larger the pool of stocks you can choose from, the higher the bar—the opportunity cost—that a new stock has to overcome to make it into the portfolio. International stocks need not be seen merely as a necessary evil for diversification—they should contribute in a real way to raising that bar, since they increase the size of the investment pool. You don't need to become the Indiana Jones of international investing by diving into developing countries like Zimbabwe or Afghanistan, where the rule of law is still in its infancy. Start with the developed countries that are in your comfort zone and then tiptoe out from there.

Chapter Twelve

Applying Darwinism to the Sales Process

Buy and Sell Is the Name of the Game

SELLING IS USUALLY AS POPULAR AS CANDY the day after Halloween. During secular bull markets selling is frowned upon as buy-and-hold turns into investing religion. And since sell violates the "hold" covenant of that religion, the investor who buys and sells is labeled as a nonbeliever, or even worse, a trader (if you say "trader" fast enough it sounds like "traitor").

In bull markets, only wimpy suckers sell as market valuations are expanding and even second-rate dogs (stocks) start looking like pedigreed cocker spaniels. Every investor is now a "long-term" investor, and sell becomes a four-letter word. But being a long-term investor is not about the longevity of your hold decisions, but rather it is an attitude. Holding a stock because you bought it is a fallacy. You should only hold a stock if the future risk-adjusted return warrants it.

Warren Buffett has been mistakenly promoted (though, I'd argue, demoted) to deity status in this buy-and-hold temple. Let's correct this mistake. Warren Buffett became a buy-and-hold investor when his portfolio and positions got big enough, pushing $60 billion, so that selling became a difficult undertaking. Being on the boards of some of his biggest holdings (like Coca-Cola and the *Washington Post*) has made selling even more difficult. In his early career, before "Oracle of Omaha" was his moniker, he was a buy-and-sell investor.

One doesn't need the benefit of hindsight to know that at over 50 times earnings Coke was tremendously overvalued in 1999. Coke, like the majority of Buffett's top public holdings (Procter & Gamble, Johnson & Johnson, and many others), did not go anywhere for a decade. Take a look at his top public holdings and tell me whether he would have done a lot better if he had sold them when they became fully valued. In most cases, that would have been a decade ago.

Emotions assault us from different directions when we face a sell decision: If it is a losing investment, we want to wait until we break even. This is the wrong attitude. Our purchase price and our sell decision should not be related (the only exception I can think of is tax selling, and even then it may be questionable). Or when it comes to selling a winner, we want to sell only at the top. Again this is the wrong attitude; the top is only apparent in hindsight, when it is usually too late.

We should sell a stock when it reaches our price or valuation target, determined at the time of purchase. We (our emotions and false goals, to be exact) are our biggest enemy when it comes to investing and especially to selling.

A proper sell discipline will make the difference between great or mediocre returns for even the best-crafted buy decisions.

An investor without a sell discipline is similar to a highway with on-ramps but no exits. The impact of losers or subpar performers in one's portfolio is usually muted in a bull market by the rise of the overall market's P/E levels. The portfolio is further helped by the performance of a few superstars—stocks whose price appreciation exceeds the wildest dreams of most investors.

Stock selection, valuation, and diversification are the building blocks of risk management in the long-only portfolio, but a sell process is the glue that holds them all together.

Things change, and not always for the better. Quality and growth—deteriorate (fundamentals worsen), making a stock a riskier and less appealing investment.

A stock appreciates, and though that's a good problem to have, it leads to parallel deterioration of that precious margin of safety.

A disciplined sell process injects a healthy dose of Darwinism (survival of the fittest) into the portfolio, weeding out the weakest stocks—the ones that have deteriorated fundamentals or diminished margin of safety—in favor of stronger ones, thus improving the portfolio and making it less risky.

A great majority of stock sell decisions in the long-term investor's portfolio fall into one of two categories:

1. The stock price has gone up, depleting the margin of safety and hindering the Valuation dimension.
2. Fundamentals (Quality, Growth, or both) have deteriorated, or you expect them to deteriorate.

Sell That Stock When?

---~---

I made my money by selling too soon.

—*Bernard Baruch*

Stocks should be purchased when the risk/reward equation is tilted in your favor and sold when that stops being the case. Stocks that became fairly valued, the ones that exhausted their margins of safety and in which expected total rate of return (earnings growth plus dividends) now fall below your expectations should be sold—period!

You buy stocks to make money. And when a stock, like a loyal pet, does what it was purchased to do—goes up—you are hesitant to part with it. It created your wealth, after all. Contemplating selling a lucrative stock that has performed feels like teaching your dog fetch and then as a reward sending him to a kennel. But a stock, unlike a pet, has no feelings to be hurt and should not be fallen in love with; it is just a tool to increase your wealth. Even when you decide to part with the stock, you want to squeeze every last penny out of it (sell at the top), but you must resist the urge.

Selling is an emotional process, often more emotional than buying. After analyzing and holding a stock for some time, you've developed an emotional connection to it. Over time, you talked to management, listened to their presentations and conference calls, studied the company's financials, scanned press releases, built models projecting company's future profitability, and more. Selling brings closure to the journey, and if the journey was successful (the price has appreciated), you don't want it to end.

But stocks are not pets. The now overvalued stock, once sold, can be bought back in the future when it starts meeting your criteria for ownership again. The stock doesn't know that you own it (an old Wall Street adage), and it will not hold a grudge against you for selling it.

Here are several strategies that should help you deal with your sell emotions.

The easiest way to deal with emotional attachment to a stock is to decide and thereby know how the game will end before it starts. Arguably, you are less emotional about a company at the time of purchase than at the time of sale. The emotions of the ownership attachment that come during the time you are holding the stock have not yet had time to develop. Setting a selling price (such as, sell at $75) or, even better, a selling valuation (such as, I'll sell this stock when it gets to a P/E of 14 or a price-to-book ratio of 1.5) at the time of purchase and strictly following through when the stock reaches the sell target should help free you from your emotions (assuming risk/reward characteristics of the stock have not changed significantly).

When a stock reaches its predetermined sell target, the sell decision should become automatic and thus unemotional, a Nike-like "Just do it!" The stock should be presumed guilty of being fairly valued, and the burden of proof should be shifted to *keeping* the stock in the portfolio, not the other way around. It should be assumed that the price or valuation target chosen at the time of purchase was rational and had a lower emotional component attached to it, thus carrying higher weight in the "to sell or not to sell" decision.

For every company in my portfolio and on my watch list I determine and write down buy, fair value, and sell P/Es.

The difficulty of selling in the sideways market is likely to be exacerbated by the fact that often you'll be selling when everybody else is buying. I suggest keeping Exhibit 2.2 in mind (frame it if you'd like) when a stock reaches its preset P/E sell target and you are having a hard time saying goodbye.

Selling When Fundamentals Have Deteriorated

With the exception of diamonds, nothing is forever, or so De Beers leads us to believe. Barbed wire that protects a company's business against competition eventually rusts. Sustainable competitive advantages are usually finite, as companies need to constantly reinvent themselves to retain them. Some companies do this more successfully than others. However, some that still have their sustainable competitive advantages have simply run out of growth.

If we look at stocks through the Quality, Valuation, and Growth prism, Valuation is usually the most volatile dimension. It is driven mainly by a company's stock-price movements, which tend to be more volatile than its fundamentals. Therefore, the Quality and Growth dimensions are usually more stable than Valuation. While Valuation may change on a dime, it usually takes much longer (months or years) for fundamental problems to develop. Exceptions to this include unexpected events such as losing an important lawsuit, invalidation of a patent, destruction by hurricane or flood, a change in regulatory environment for the industry, and so on.

I'm not a real movie star. I've still got the same wife I started out with twenty-eight years ago.

—*Will Rogers*

At the risk of being called a "stockosexual," I'll say the following: Marry your stocks, but with a prenuptial agreement.

Though marrying stocks—falling in love, staying by their side (not selling) for better or worse, in sickness and in health—is not wise in any market. In a sideways market, however, it could well prove fatal to your portfolio. In a perfect world, a stock-investing paradise, we would buy a portfolio of great companies that would grow consistently, and their prices would appreciate smoothly in line with their earnings, thus maintaining an appropriate margin of safety at all times. Their businesses would never change, nor would the competitive structure of the industries in which they operate. And their management, being super-humans, would always make wise decisions—wouldn't that be nice? Then we could safely marry all of our stocks and keep them until death do us part. Unfortunately (or maybe not), investing is not a utopian paradise.

You need to strike a balance between excessive, pro-miscuous stock dating—selling after one bad joke—and marriage in its traditional sense, namely forever. I don't want to cheapen investing by comparing it to a Hollywood-type marriage that just lasts a few weeks or months. But there is a lesson we should learn from our movie stars: Have a prenuptial agreement.

We should buy stocks in the hope of staying married to them forever, but knowing that there is a chance it won't work out.

The terms of your prenup should be specific: You will identify and closely track important variables that consti-tute a scorecard of a company's fundamental performance such as sales growth, net margins, return on capital, or some industry-specific variables. For retailers, for instance, these variables could be same-store sales growth, inventory turnover, sales per square foot, operating margin, losses due to theft and spoilage, and so on.

Once these variables stop meeting your expectations, the stock should be put on "double secret probation" to see if it improves and should be closely watched. If these variables don't improve in a set time frame such as a few quarters, it's time for a divorce and the stock should be sold.

If the movie *Animal House* taught us anything, it is the importance of "double secret probation"—singling out a stock and subjecting it to a higher-priority, under-the-magnifying-glass analysis. You should take a proactive approach to selling stocks before problems escalate. Keep fundamental underperformers on a shorter leash, sell sooner, and give less time for the company to fix things. In a sideways market a short leash is doubly important.

I am not advocating setting quarter-by-quarter earnings targets, since that may prove to be a fruitless exercise. Meeting or beating quarterly estimates by a penny, quarter after quarter, is not necessarily an indication of a company's quality or superior fundamental performance. Creative accounting has helped a lot of companies to look good in a very consistent manner, only later to be found achieving their quarterly miracles by massaging numbers, or worse yet, by cooking their books.

Set fundamental performance targets or goals. When the company stops meeting those goals, it should be put on double secret probation. You should consider reviewing your assumptions. If they were incorrect, then evaluate whether the company is still a buy under the revised assumptions. One setback doesn't make the trend; thus double secret probation works as a prioritizing tool for companies that you have to watch like a hawk. Similar to the company reaching a price or valuation target, once a company makes it onto your double secret probation list, its presumption of innocence is forfeited—it is now guilty until proven otherwise!

Disassociate Yourself from Previous Decisions

The rare ability to draw back from one's circumstances and view them at arm's length, as a stranger might view things, is a valuable skill indeed. A famous example from the mid-1980s was Intel facing new competition from Japan in commoditized memory chips—Intel's bread and butter at the time. This new development sent Intel from making $198 million in 1984 to making a mere $2 million in 1985. Andy Grove, CEO of Intel, agonized for weeks over the dilemma, as he recounted in *Only the Paranoid Survive* (Doubleday Currency, 1996):

> I looked out the window at the Ferris wheel of the Great
> America amusement park revolving in the distance when
> I turned back to Gordon [Moore—Intel's founder], and I
> asked, "If we got kicked out and the board brought in a
> new CEO, what do you think he would do?" Gordon
> answered without hesitation, "He would get us out of
> memories." I stared at him, numb, then said, "Why
> shouldn't you and I walk out the door, come back, and
> do it ourselves?"

Intel refocused its efforts on microprocessors and
became one of the most profitable companies in the world,
with sales exceeding $40 billion and net income exceeding
$10 billion in 2010.

By taking an outsider point of view—"If we got kicked
out and the board brought in a new CEO, what do you
think he would do?"—Andy Grove dumped years' worth
of emotional baggage—the financial and emotional costs
that had been sunk into an obsolete product strategy—
and thus came to a difficult but critically important decision. By looking at the problem from an outsider's
perspective, he was able to gain clarity; a new CEO would
not have the baggage, so decisions would be forward, not
backward looking.

This example is useful in decision making in many
facets of our lives, but it is particularly useful when it
comes to investments, and especially selling. The baggage of past decisions often haunts us when we attempt

to make sell decisions. Selling a stock that is experiencing deteriorating fundamentals forces us to admit that buying that stock was a mistake. We have to accept that not every decision we make will work out. This is just the reality of investments. Paraphrasing my friend Todd Harrison, "If there wasn't risk, it would be called winning, not investing!"

Understanding our own behavior when it comes to making investment decisions is critically important. I said it before, and I'll say it again: Emotions are our worst investing enemy after all, since they lead us to do the opposite of what we should be doing. One of the behavioral traps we fall into is anchoring our current views to our past decisions. For example, the need to feel good about ourselves often causes us to base buy and sell decisions on a past stock price. We later anchor our sell decisions to our purchase price—if the stock is now down, we hold on hoping to break even. Or we anchor our minds to a stock's recent high or low.

Let's take a look at this example: A company comes out with bad news, and before you even have a chance to read the press release—boom, the stock drops. Or, in a similar situation, the stock was drifting down on no news, and it had declined significantly (in tandem with the market or by itself) since you bought it, but you haven't sold because you thought nothing had changed. Then a new piece of information comes out—the company loses a major contract or competition took a bigger market share away than you expected. You must try to step outside of yourself and ask, "If a new person were to manage my portfolio, the one who did not buy this stock, what would he do?" This attitude should liberate you from your past decisions and let you focus on the present and the future. What do you do? You pretend you don't own the stock, and you revalue the company. If you come up with a fair value above today's price, you do nothing and keep holding it. If you discover that, despite the price drop, the fair value of the company is at the today's price or below, you forget about pride and sell.

Chapter Thirteen

You Are Not As Dumb—or Smart— As You Think

Moral Support for Buying and Selling in a Sideways Market

SECULAR SIDEWAYS MARKETS ARE COMPRISED of many cyclical bull and bear markets (just as a reminder, take a look again at Exhibit 2.2). Though cyclical bull and bear markets can provide great buying and selling opportunities, our emotions will try to get in the way between us and the right decisions. Markets will constantly try to brainwash us into doing the opposite of what we should be doing. I hope this chapter provides an antidote to this as it contains two missives. Read the first one during cyclical bear markets and the second during the cyclical bull markets. Good luck!

You Are Not as Dumb as You Think (Psychotherapy for Cyclical Bear Markets)

Lately, I've been getting this nagging feeling that everything I touch turns to dirt. Every time I buy a stock that is already down a lot, the one that my analysis leads me to believe is cheaper than dirt, it declines more. Did I completely lose my ability to value stocks? Did I start ignoring Will Rogers' advice to buy stocks that go up, and if they don't go up, don't buy them?

No, I didn't get dumber, and my stock-picking skills haven't diminished. I was simply a willing participant in the latest cyclical bear market. Bear markets make you feel dumber than you are, the same way bull markets make you feel smarter than you are.

Feeling dumb makes you do the opposite of what you should be doing. Fear and pain—yes, continued losses cause a lot of pain—are dangerous things because they can make you and me panic, lose confidence, and do the opposite of what we should be doing. To alleviate pain we sell, we react, we default to the only asset that made us money so far in the bear market—cash! When you cannot find a stock with a long-term superior risk/reward profile, then cash is King with a capital K. However, during a cyclical bear market, cash slowly loses its crown, as great companies are thrown out the window with the junky ones. You have to actively remind yourself of the eight-letter word *T-O-M-O-R-R-O-W!* Yes, tomorrow. Think of the lyrics from the musical *Annie*.

Of course, we don't know if tomorrow is really tomorrow or five years from now. But investing is a marathon, not a sprint—don't let a bear market turn you into a sprinter. First of all, remind yourself that you are not as dumb as your portfolio makes you feel. You have occasionally bought a stock that made you money. This is what I do: I pull out a chart of a stock on which I made a boatload of money, or of one that I sold for the right reasons before it declined. I do this with pleasure, trying to relive my smart days. We all have these stocks, the ones we nailed. We tend to forget about them during bear market phases. But I suggest you remember them now, when you feel lonely and miserable, so you'll have more of these names to remember in the future, since cash will not bring the pleasure of victory in the long run. The cyclical bull market is still there; it is just hiding under the ugly sentiment of the cyclical bear market. Believe me, it will show its happy face. It is just a matter of time.

In a bear market, it is easy to forget about buying. Selling is a much easier decision to make. Every time you buy a stock you look dumb, because it usually goes down afterward. I recently bought a couple of incredibly cheap stocks and, of course, they declined. I don't feel smart about these buys right now. However, a while back, I analyzed these companies, figured out what they were worth, determined an appropriate margin of safety, and got my buy prices. The stocks declined, but fundamentals had not changed, so I bought the stocks.

You cannot worry about marking the bottom in every buy. My objective is not to buy at the bottom and sell at the top. No, my objective is to buy a great company when it is cheap and sell it when it is fairly valued. I suggest you do the same. Will Rogers' advice is great, but unfortunately I have yet to meet a human being who has figured out how to apply it in real life. No, you are not as dumb as bear markets make you feel.

You Are Not as Smart as You Think (Psychotherapy for Cyclical Bull Markets)

Lately, I've been getting this powerful feeling that everything I touch turns to gold. Every time I buy a stock, it goes up. Did I finally figure out the stock market game? Did I find the secret to applying Will Rogers' advice?

No, I didn't get much smarter, and my stock-picking skills haven't improved much over the past year. I was simply a willing participant in the latest cyclical bull market. A bull market makes you feel smarter than you are the same way a bear market makes you feel dumber. Feeling smart makes you do the opposite of what you should be doing. The euphoria of the golden touch is a dangerous thing, because it can make us careless. We forget about risk, since we haven't seen it in a while, and we focus only on rewards. You have to actively remind yourself of the four-letter word *R-I-S-K!*

How do you do that? My favorite way is to remind myself how dumb I am. I pull out an annual report of a company on which I lost a boatload of money and masochistically try to read it from cover to cover, reliving my dumbness.

We all have these stocks, the ones we lost a lot of money on, because we were overconfident. We tend to forget about them during bull market phases. But I suggest you remember them now, so you'll have fewer of those names to remember in the future. Risk is still there; it is just hiding under the joyful sentiment of the bull market. Believe me, it will show its ugly face. It is just a matter of time.

In a bull market, it is easy to forget about selling discipline and turn into a "buy and forget to sell" investor.

Every time you sell a stock you look dumb, because it usually goes up afterward. I recently sold a bunch of stocks at their fair value and, completely ignoring my actions, they went higher. I don't feel smart about those decisions. However, when I bought the stocks, I set sell P/Es, and when they approached their value, I quickly reviewed their fundamentals, they had not changed much, so I sold them.

You cannot worry about marking the top in every sell. My objective is not to buy at the bottom and sell at the top. No, my objective is to buy a great company when it is cheap and to sell it when it is fairly valued! I suggest you do the same.

Chapter Fourteen

On a Scavenger Hunt
for Stocks

*Once You've Sold, What Should
You Buy?*

STRICT SELL DISCIPLINE WILL INCREASE PORTFOLIO turn-over, and replacing stocks that are on the way out with new ones will become a priority. This creates the need for a continuous new-idea discovery process. Here are some suggestions on how to find new stocks.

Map the Market

Contrarian investors are usually drawn to the sectors that are not hitting all-time highs but are instead staring into the abyss of multiweek, -month, or -year lows. An easy way to identify an entire group of stocks the market has dumped in favor of a new fling is by looking at exchange-traded funds (ETFs).

ETFs provide an elegant and easy way to map the global markets, as they are slicing and dicing them every conceivable and some previously inconceivable ways—by sector; stock characteristic (market capitalization, P/E, dividend yield); investment style (value, growth); asset class (stocks, bonds, gold, oil, currency); CEO's height and weight (okay, I made that one up)—covering the globe in every plausible way.

Periodic review of ETF performance provides a quick but useful global intelligence report on what different pockets of the market are doing, helping you to be selective about where you spend your energy looking for ideas and enabling you to spend your time in places where opportunities are more likely to exist.

Use Screens

Stock screening is to value investing what apple pie is to America. Stock cheapness is quantifiable, thus value investors screen. Here I'll just mention some of my favorite screens. All of these can be supplemented with your own qualifiers, throwing in your own magic by adding debt ratios, dividend yield, return on capital thresholds, or anything else that would help you find companies that fit your approach.

The Little Book That Beats the Market screen: This stock screen was introduced in a book by Joel Greenblatt appropriately named *The Little Book That Beats the Market* (John Wiley & Sons, 2006). In this stock screen, companies are ranked by P/E (lower P/E gets a lower score) and by return on equity (ROE, higher ROE gets a lower score), and then scores are added together. The top candidates on the list—the ones that have the lowest scores—are your latest and greatest ideas. This simple but brilliant formula has beaten the market since the 1980s.

Low price to anything screens: These are the most popular screens, where you simply look for cheap stocks; the lower the number, the better. Here are just some variations that come to mind: P/E, price to cash flow, price to book, price to EBITDA, price to dividend, and price to sales; "anything" could really be anything. You can make adjustments to price by calculating a company's enterprise value (market value less cash plus debt).

Hitting the bottom screen: This screens for stocks that are hitting multiweek, -month, or -year lows.

Low price to normalized anything screen: The low price to anything screen may miss stocks that have suffered a short-term setback, or are on the wrong side of the economic cycle, or simply took an accounting charge. Company earnings or cash flows will be depressed below their normal level and the stock will fall through the price to anything screen, since its P/E or price to cash flow, for instance, will be overstated. To run a P/E screen, you should compute P/E not based on current earnings, but by taking an average net profit margin over three or five years and applying it to current sales, or average sales over the same time period.

Net-net stocks screen: This is a classic Benjamin Graham screen where you try to buy stocks as close to, or preferably below, their net current assets (current assets less all liabilities including debt and preferred stock). Or you could look for companies that trade close to their net cash (cash including short-term investments less all interest-bearing debt).

Analyst sentiment screen: Stock prices are impacted by Wall Street analysts' recommendations. It is common for a stock to be up or down several percentage points on changes in analyst recommendations from buy to sell, hold to buy, and so on. A stock that has every piece of bad news priced into it usually has a lot of analysts' disapproving sell ratings stamped all over it.

There is more than one way to screen for analyst sentiment. You can calculate the percentage of sell and hold recommendations to total recommendations and then screen or sort for the highest percentages. For example, if a stock has seven sells, two holds, and one buy recommendation by sell-side analysts, you may interpret that as a 70-percent sell recommendation (7 out of 10) or a 90 percent non-buy recommendation (7 sells plus 2 holds out of 10). Hold recommendations are usually weak sell recommendations. They provide a way for an analyst to tell investors not to buy the stock but at the same time for him not to end up on the company's we-hate-that-ungrateful-analyst list.

Borrow

Good writers borrow from other writers. Great writers steal from them outright.

—*Sam Seaborn*, The West Wing

Most of us have value investors in mind whose investment approaches we admire and can relate to, and if you don't, now is a good time to start making a list of these investors and to start following their holdings. The only rub here is that they have to manage over $100 million.

The $100 million requirement is not because I think that anybody who invests less than that should not be followed, but because Securities and Exchange Commission (SEC) rules require institutional (non–mutual fund) investors that manage over $100 million to disclose their stock holdings on a quarterly basis; thus their holdings can be followed.

The SEC Web site, though improved over the years, is still a maze when it comes to uncovering needed financial documents. I have been using GuruFocus.com to find the latest holdings by institutional investors. It's useful and easy to navigate.

Looking at the holdings of other value managers is really just another screen for attractive opportunities that are not caught by traditional screens. It can be a start but not the end of your research process. You still want to do your own research, the same process you would have conducted if you had come to the idea on your own. If you mindlessly borrowed ideas without doing your own research, you had would not know what to do when things don't go as you had planned (the stock declines or fundamentals deteriorate or both).

Notice I suggested following the holdings of investors "whose investment approaches we admire and can relate to." I did not suggest that you follow investors who have great track records. There are several reasons for this: First, their track records could simply be random phenomena—they've taken a lot of risk and luck was on their side. Looking at track records alone is not enough. Second, even if success was due to an excellent process, it may not fit *your* process. We should always be willing to learn from others, but in the end we still have to remain who we are.

Chapter Fifteen

Farewell, Blissful Ignorance

~

Why You Can't Stick Your Head in the Sand When It Comes to Global Issues

DURING THE 1980s AND 1990s, ignorance was bliss. The global economy was growing nicely, and analyzing it, or even paying attention to market cycles, seemed like a waste of time, since the economy came in only three flavors: good, great, and awesome. Even if you misread the flavor, your downside was that you'd just make a little less money. Value investors prided themselves on being bottom-up-only analysts (focusing only on analyzing and valuing individual stocks), while top-down (making investment decisions by looking only at the macro picture) became unfashionable, as it was looked upon as market timing.

Prolonged and virtually uninterrupted growth brought complacency, excesses, and debt. Bottom-up-only analysis worked until it stopped working, as investors discovered during the recent crisis that the global economy can also come in additional flavors: bad, horrible, and downright nasty. Today, the cost of misreading the economy is much higher. (I know the above statement may sound a bit over the top, but over the years I have read and listened to dozens of interviews with famous and successful investors who declared that they do bottom-up-only analysis and don't pay attention to the economy.)

When we buy a stock we are buying a stream of future cash flows. By doing bottom-up-only analysis, an investor implicitly assumes that external factors (the winds and hurricanes of the global economy) have no impact on these cash flows. That is a brave and careless assumption. I suggest a 360-degree (or head-to-toe if you like) analysis—mix bottom-up with insights you get from top-down analysis.

I didn't just say *economy*, I said *global economy*. As we painfully discovered during the most recent financial crisis, our national and global economies are more interconnected than ever. Therefore, in this chapter we'll focus not just on the United States, we'll also take a look at what is happening in the world's second and third largest economies, China and Japan.

To understand the future we need to very briefly revisit the past. Over several decades preceding the Great Recession, consumer debt-to-GDP was steadily on the rise, going from 50 percent in the early 1980s to 70 percent in the late 1990s. Then came the housing boom—consumer borrowing went vertical, helped by rising home prices and low interest rates. In a span of less than 10 years consumer debt-to-GDP went from around 70 percent to more than 100 percent—a tremendous increase, since it took 20 years to change from 50 to 70 percent in the 1980s and 1990s.

False Axioms and Consequences

Let me introduce the concept of the *false axiom*. An axiom is a proposition that is unproved but considered to be self-evident and not requiring proof. Any axiom that relies on extrapolated data is only a belief or an assumption that may, over time, prove to be false. In the United States a false axiom was that real estate prices never decline nationwide—and this supposed axiom was supported by more than 50 years of hard data. This rather remarkable condition persisted for so long that all market players believed in it. Everyone from the Federal Reserve to banks and credit agencies thought that it was an axiom; but lo and behold, it was a false axiom, and belief in it led to overbuilding, overcapacity, and over-indebtedness.

The Great Recession waltzed in, to the great surprise of homeowners, the Fed, the banks—everyone discovered that house prices don't always go up, but can also decline. The financial sector, the lifeblood of our economy, started to drown in the sea of bad debt. Suddenly, the financial sector, which for decades had been singing hymns of independence from government regulation, was begging government to come in and bail it out. As the troubles in the financial sector started to spill into the real economy, the government felt it had no choice, and the bailouts and stimuli began.

Today it is hard to take a walk through our economy and not meet the friendly Uncle Sam; he is everywhere. He's buying long-term bonds and thereby keeping long-term rates artificially low. Since he took over the defunct (for all practical purposes) Fannie and Freddie, he himself is the U.S. mortgage market. Of course, our dear uncle is also on the hook for their losses.

Banks, though they won't admit it in public, are benefitting tremendously from Uncle Sam's intervention, as they are the veins through which he injects stimulus into the economy. Plus, his involvement in the housing market helps banks generate enormous fees, props up home prices, and lowers bank losses on mortgages. But it doesn't stop there, because bank profitability is also boosted (at the expense of savers) by nearly zero short-term interest rates that allow banks to earn healthy interest-rate spreads.

Our dear Uncle Sam rolls in style, he doesn't know how to bail out or stimulate on the cheap; oh no, the U.S. government debt (at least that portion of it, which appeared on the balance sheet) leapt from around 60 percent of GDP pre-Great Recession to over 100 percent in 2010. The party of overleveraged consumers has now been crashed by overleveraged government.

To understand the consequences of the Great Recession, consider this analogy. The U.S. economy is like a marathon runner who runs too hard and hurts himself but has another race to run. So he's injected with some serious, industrial-quality steroids, and away he goes. As the steroids kick in, his pace accelerates as if the injury never happened. He's up and running, so he *must* be okay—this is the impression we get, judging from his speed and his progress. What we don't see is what is

behind this athlete's terrific performance—the steroids—
or in the case of our economy, the stimulus.

Of course, we can keep our fingers crossed and hope
the runner has recovered from his injury and what we see
is what we get—the athlete is at the top of his game—but
there are problems with this thinking. Let's address them
one by one.

- Serious steroid intake exaggerates true performance. Stimulus creates an appearance of stability and growth, but a lot of it is teetering on a
  very weak foundation of government intervention.
  (Think what will happen to banks and the housing
  market if government walks away.)
- Steroids are addictive; once we get used to their
  effects it is hard to give them up. When the first
  home-buyer tax credit expired, it was extended to
  anyone with the patriotic ambition to buy a house.
  It is hard to give up stimulus, because the immediate consequences are too painful, but long-term
  gain has to be purchased with short-term pain.
- The longer we take steroids the less effective they
  are. As we'll discuss in a few pages, Japan was on
  the stimulus bandwagon for more than a decade,
  and with the exception of government debt tripling,
  Japan has nothing to show for it—the economy

is mired in the same rut it was when the stimulus marathon started.

- Finally, steroids damage the athlete's body and stimulus comes with significant side effects—higher future taxes and increased government debt, which bring interest rates up and consequently result in below-average economic growth. The same tailwind of increased debt that helped to propel economic growth turns into a headwind as consumer and eventually government deleveraging shaves off additional points from economic growth.

The hopes that we'll transition from government steroid injections back to an economy running on its own are overly optimistic; there is just too much stimulus and too much debt in the economy for that to happen.

Japan: Past the Point of No Return

I never thought I'd draw parallels between what is going on in the United States and what transpired in Japan over the last 20 years, but with every new stimulus and inching up of national debt we are resembling Japan more and more. Unfortunately for Japan, as you'll see, it is past the point of no return—it will go from deflation to hyperinflation. For now, the United States still has a chance to avoid Japan's fate.

Japan's economic fate is a grey swan.* Never heard of a grey swan? Well it is a not-so-distant cousin of the black swan, which signifies a rare, significant, and *unpredictable* event. However, what is taking place in Japan is rare and significant but *predictable*; we don't know *when* it will play out, but we know it will happen.

The prelude to Japan's current crisis occurred in the early 1990s when its housing and stock market bubbles popped and the Japanese economy plunged into a recession. For the next 20 years, flashy names like *Fiscal Structural Reform Act*, *Emergency Employment Measures*, and *Policy Measures of Economic Rebirth* were trotted out year after year as the government cut taxes, increased spending, and borrowed money to finance itself. Once or twice the government found fiscal religion and raised taxes; however, the economy stuttered and taxes were again lowered, and another sorry chapter in the stimulus story was written.

Today, 20 years into perpetual stimulus, the Japanese economy is beset by the same rot it was two decades ago, and the ratio of debt to GDP is over 200 percent, double the rates of the United States and Germany and second only to Zimbabwe.

---

*Nassim Taleb, one of my favorite thinkers, brought both black and grey swans to life in his books *Fooled by Randomness* (Random House, 2008) and *The Black Swan* (Random House, 2007).

A country that has ballooning debt needs to have an expanding economy to help it outgrow its debt burden. Economic growth is driven by two factors, productivity and population growth. Though the Japanese economy may continue to reap the benefits of productivity, population growth is not in the cards.

Japan has one of the oldest populations in the developed world. Every fourth Japanese is over 65 years of age, and Japan's population numbers are on the decline. Due to cultural mores, workers are compensated not on merit but on time spent at the company, so young adults marry later in life and have fewer kids later. This, in part, explains why the Japanese birth rate is one of the lowest in the world, a meager 1.2 per woman. (To maintain a constant population level, an average woman needs to give birth to 2.1 children—one to replace her, one her husband/partner, and 0.1 to counter pre-childbearing mortality.)

Unlike the United States, which sees constant population growth due to immigration, there is little immigration into Japan. Though its debt is ballooning, GDP is unlikely to grow (more likely to decline), and thus debt-to-GDP and debt per capita will only rise.

Though debt has tripled over the last two decades, Japanese government spending on interest payments has not changed; in fact, it even declined a little in the mid-2000s. This happened because the average interest rate paid on government debt declined from over 6 percent in the 1990s to 1.4 percent in 2009. This is about to change. Historically, over 90 percent of Japanese government-issued debt was consumed internally by its citizens, directly or through its pension system. In the 1990s the savings rate was very high, pushing mid-teens. However, as people get older they retire, start drawing down their savings and pensions, and savings rates decline. Today the Japanese savings rate is approaching zero and will likely go negative in the not too distant future.

The Japanese economy operates on the false axiom that the government will always be able to borrow at low interest rates. Twenty years of data support this axiom, but continued reliance on this axiom will lead to its violation. As internal demand for debt evaporates—and this is occurring already—and new debt is issued and/or maturing debt is replaced, Japanese savers will not be there to buy it. The Japanese government will have to start hocking its debt outside Japan, in a more realistic world where interest rates are a lot higher. Japanese 10-year treasuries that are yielding half of U.S. or German bonds of the same maturities will not have a chance. Japan will have to offer rates far in excess of their U.S. and German counterparts. Though they have their own problems, the United States and Germany still have much lower indebtedness and superior demographic growth profiles.

The Japanese stimulative, low-interest policy landed the country in a debt trap. It cannot afford higher interest rates, and low interest rates are not stimulative to the economy, not anymore. It gets worse: In 2009 more than a quarter of Japan's tax revenue went toward interest payments. If their interest expense doubles (if the average borrowing rate goes up from 1.4 to 2.8 percent), the increase in the cost of debt will equal the size of the Japanese budgets for education, science, and national defense spending combined. Higher interest rates will likely trigger debt downgrades, which will only drive borrowing costs higher.

❧

By a continuing process of inflation, government can confiscate, secretly and unobserved, an important part of the wealth of their citizens.

—*John Maynard Keynes*

Higher taxes and the austerity measures that will undoubtedly follow, combined with higher interest rates, will slow down the economy further and drive Japan towards insolvency. Unlike European countries that socialized their currencies and cannot print money on their own, Japan has complete control over its currency printing press. Also, unlike Greece, which due to its size could be bailed out by Germany and friends, with a bit of help from the ever-willing IMF, Japan is too big to be bailed out. Defaulting on its own debt, especially when the majority of it is owned by its own citizens, is a political impossibility. This is why governments that have control over their currencies don't default, they print. And print they will in Japan! Decades of deflation will turn into hyperinflation, which will destroy the purchasing power of citizens' savings and eventually collapse the yen.

The consequences of what is slowly but surely unraveling in Japan are important to U.S. investors because these consequences will not stay in Japan but will spill into the United States and the rest of the world. Japan is the second largest foreign holder of U.S. government debt, and its demand for our fine paper will decline. Most likely, Japan will start selling U.S. Treasuries; and to make things worse, Japan will start competing with us, not just in cars and electronics, but for buyers of sovereign government debt. Japan will export inflation, inflation will rise globally, and so will interest rates.

China: The Mother of All Grey Swans

Of course, Japan is not the only large holder of U.S. Treasuries; it shares this privilege with China, who in 2010 beat out Japan for the title of the second largest economy in the world, having grown into a grey swan of enormous proportions.

Westerners look at China with envy; it can do nothing wrong. Its economy grew at 10 percent for a decade without skipping a beat. During the global financial crisis, while the world economy was contracting, China's growth slowed; but it was still growing in mid-single digits. It seems that Chinese "Confucian capitalism"—a concoction of an authoritarian regime and a free-market economy perversely intertwined with a government-controlled economy, supersized by the enormous 1.3 billion population—is superior to our touchy-feely, garden-variety democracy and capitalism. But don't be in a hurry to trade in our political and economic system; the Chinese grass is not as green as it appears.

To understand the Chinese economy we need to divide our analysis into three distinct periods: the decade prior to 2008, the period of the worldwide financial crisis, and from the end of the financial crisis to 2010.

Rewind the clock a decade to the late 1990s. At that time the Chinese government chose a policy of growth at any cost. A lot of peasants moved to the cities in search of higher-paying jobs during the go-go times. Because China lacks the social safety net of the developed world, unemployed people aren't just inconvenienced by the loss of their jobs, they starve; hungry people don't complain, they riot and cause political unrest.

In the movie *Speed*, if Keanu Reeves didn't keep the bus above 50 mph, it would explode. Well, China is like a bus with 1.3 billion people aboard and the Chinese Communist Party at the wheel—if the economy doesn't sustain its high growth speed, the outcome will be catastrophic. Once you look at what's taking place in the Chinese economy through that lens, the decisions of its leaders start making sense or at least become understandable.

To achieve high growth, China has kept its currency, the renminbi, at artificially low levels against the dollar—this helped already cheap Chinese-made goods stay even cheaper than those of China's global competitors. Thus, China turned into a significant exporter to the developed economies.

Normally, if free-market economic forces were at work, the renminbi would have appreciated and the U.S. dollar would have declined. However, if China let its currency appreciate, its exports would have become more expensive, the demand for Chinese products would have declined, and its economy wouldn't have grown at

10 percent a year. Also, China holds close to a trillion dollars worth of U.S. Treasuries, so appreciation of the renminbi against the dollar would diminish the value of China's dollar reserves. The more China sells to the United States, the more dollars it accumulates and the more U.S. Treasuries it buys, driving our interest rates down.

However, companies and countries that grow at very high rates for a long time will inevitably suffer from late-stage growth obesity—inefficiencies that are a by-product of high growth rates sustained over a long period. Though Chinese growth in the past was high, in its later stages the quality of growth has been low. For instance, China built the second largest shopping mall in the world, the New South China Mall; today (2010) it's still vacant. China also built a lavish city for a million people called Ordos; today it's a ghost town.

In the midst of financial crisis, Chinese exports were down more than 25 percent, the tonnage of goods shipped through its railroads was down by double digits, and its electricity consumption fell like a rock. However, according to the Chinese government, China magically sustained mid-single-digit GDP growth. Who would you rather believe, the Chinese government or hard, common-sense data? The Chinese government goes to great lengths to maintain appearances, including censoring media and jailing those who write anti-government articles, to keep its ideology going. The Chinese government lied about economic growth, as independent, nongovernment statistics show. Like the rest of the world, the Chinese economy was contracting during the financial crisis.

Fast-forward to 2010. The United States and Europe, the consumers of Chinese-made goods, are overleveraged and now deleveraging, unemployment is high, the banks have got religion and aren't lending, and there's not much demand for loans anyway (except by the U.S. government). You might think the Chinese economy would be growing at a lower rate. But no, China is growing like the financial crisis never happened—its growth rate is approaching 10 percent again.

Though this growth appears to be authentic—electricity consumption is back up—it is not sustainable growth, because it is based on an unprecedented stimulus package and extraordinary government involvement in the economy.

In the midst of the financial crisis, in late 2008, Beijing firehosed a $568 billion (14 percent of GDP) stimulus into the Chinese economy. That's enormous! The story gets even more interesting. Unlike Western democracies, whose central banks can pump a lot of money into the financial system but can't force banks to lend or consumers and corporations to spend, China can achieve both at lightning speed. The government controls the banks, thus it can make them lend, and it can force state-owned enterprises (one-third of the economy) to borrow and to spend. Also, because the rules of law and human and property rights are nascent in its economic and political system, China can spend infrastructure project money very fast.

Government is horrible at allocating large amounts of capital, especially at the speed it is done in China. Political decisions (driven by the goal of full employment) are often uneconomical, and corruption and cronyism result in projects that destroy value.

Infrastructure and real estate projects are where you get your biggest bang for the buck, if your goal is to maintain employment, because they require a lot of unskilled labor; this is where in the past a lot of Chinese money was spent. The enormous stimulus amplified problems that already existed before the financial crisis.

Chinese spare capacity in cement is greater than the combined consumption of the United States, Japan, and India. Also, Chinese idle production of steel is greater than the production capacity of Japan and South Korea combined, according to Pivot Capital Management ("China's Investment Boom: The Great Leap into the Unknown"). Similarly disturbing statistics exist for many other industrial commodities. Jim Chanos, a famous short seller known for due diligence, made an interesting observation on CNBC's *Squawk Box* in January 2010: "There's currently 30 billion square feet of Chinese real estate in the works, which would work out to a 5×5 cubicle for every man, woman, and child in the country." The false axiom in China is that the economy will always enjoy strong growth. And this also explains why they keep building skyscrapers even though the adjacent ones are still vacant. We have to remember that economic bubbles are usually just a good thing taken too far. Yes, China has an enormous bubble on its hands.

Crime and Punishment

To sum up, on the global economic front, we are facing two types of problems: First, our macro environment is swarming with grey swans, and second, a lot of the past earnings growth for many U.S. and foreign companies came at the expense of the future, and that future is today.

Chinese economic growth was a very important force pushing the global economy out of the Great Recession; however, growth that is predicated on massive forced lending is unsustainable and dangerous. As Chinese growth slows, China will turn from the wind in the sails of the global economy to its anchor. As investors, to assess the future we look to the past—we study companies' profit margins and past sales growth, along with the economic relationships and conditions of the last few decades. But today we are sitting at an interesting juncture; past success in many industries has been achieved at the expense of future growth. We should be asking what a company's true earnings power will be after tailwinds turn into headwinds. It is prudent to minimize your exposure to stocks of cyclical industries that were in vogue over the last decade (think commodities, materials, industrials). We should increase the required margin of safety for these stocks to compensate for uncertainty in "E"—earnings. Decline in demand for commodities will disproportionately impact commodity-exporting nations (think Canada, Russia, Brazil, Australia, the Middle East) that were significant beneficiaries of the past demand. If your portfolio has exposure to these nations, you are indirectly exposed to the Chinese grey swan.

This point is important, thus I'll repeat: In our stock valuations, our required margin of safety needs to be increased to compensate for the P/E compression that is brought to us by sideways markets *and* for the uncertainty in "E" that is caused by all the giant grey swans splashing around in the global economy.

GMO, a very respected investment firm run by Jeremy Grantham, did a study and found that high-quality companies outperform lower-quality ones during times of weak or negative economic growth and uncertainty by a significant margin. I defined what constitutes a high-quality company in Chapter 5, but this definition needs further clarification for today's very uncertain economic environment. Since both inflation and deflation are possible scenarios down the road, to combat either one you must own companies that can raise prices during inflation and at least maintain them in case of deflation. They also need to have solid, debt-free balance sheets. During extended periods of deflation, if a company carries a lot of non-callable debt, which is a fixed cost, it suffers—its revenues decline but fixed costs don't. Inflation is a friend of a company that has a debt-rich balance sheet, when revenues rise faster than fixed costs. In addition, Japanese and Chinese declines in appetite for our debt will boost our interest rates, and this may happen with or without inflation. This will have less of a negative impact on companies that have little or no debt to refinance. I err on the side of conservative balance sheets, even if it means that I'll make less money in the inflationary scenario.

How does this gloomy macro picture impact the sideways market? Sideways markets are a tug of war between two forces: earnings growth and P/E compression. Global and U.S. growth over the next decade will be lower than we experienced over the last few decades. As long as earnings are growing, even if at a slower rate than in the past (let's say 2 to 3 percent versus 5 to 6 percent previously), then the market is likely to continue its sideways journey, though it may turn into a longer one. However, if over the next decade the U.S. economy fails to produce earnings growth, then P/E compression will win this tug of war and our cowardly lion market will turn into a bear one.

In the early 2000s my firm, Investment Management Associates, Inc., owned stock of MBIA, a municipal bond insurance company. MBIA had a beautiful business model: It collected insurance premiums from municipalities to insure their bonds, municipalities rarely defaulted, and MBIA was coining money. However, the municipal bond market stopped growing and MBIA wanted growth. It started to insure other, more complex (and what appeared to be much riskier) bonds. My partner at Investment Management Associates, Michael Conn, decided that this new business came at a much higher risk, and we sold the stock.

For almost seven years that decision appeared to be wrong, as MBIA kept minting money and those risks Michael was afraid of did not materialize. Then 2008 came along, the housing market declined, the exotic mortgage bonds MBIA insured collapsed, and the company was on the hook to make bond investors whole. (At this point all MBIA troubles were outside of its municipal bond portfolio.) However, MBIA did not have sufficient reserves to pay them and the stock collapsed.

Hope and self-deception are not a strategy, at least not a successful one. In analyzing a stock or an economy we seek to get as close to the truth as possible. But that is not enough; we also need to have the mental aptitude and fortitude to act on our findings, no matter how inconvenient or shocking they may be. Investing is a probabilities game—even a likely event doesn't have 100 percent certainty. Also, just because the risk has not materialized yet doesn't mean that it won't show its ugly face in the future. Yes, it took seven years for MBIA to blow up. Neither Michael nor I fretted when the MBIA stock went higher after we sold it; nor did we celebrate when it blew up. We had moved on to something else.

After reading this chapter you may be inclined to address me as Dr. Doom. I don't have a Ph.D., thus I can only be called Mr. Doom—but I am not that either. A joke told by Warren Buffett comes to mind: A patient, after hearing from a doctor that he has cancer, tells the doctor, "Doc, I don't have enough money for the surgery, but could I pay you to touch up the x-ray?" We should be on the lookout for risks. They'll often look like grey swans, and we must constantly ask ourselves what we can do to avoid them (or how we can benefit from them) in our portfolios. We accept the fact that we'll never get the timing just right, but we'll be handsomely rewarded for our patience and risk avoidance when the grey stuff hits the fan. Call me Mr. Realist.

Chapter Sixteen

Think Different

A Different Approach to Risk and Diversification

YOU CAN PROBABLY SAVE A GOOD-SIZE forest by recycling academic papers on risk and diversification. These concepts are drummed into students' heads in academia, but their practical application is usually spoiled by long formulas awash in Greek symbols. I kept that in mind and wrote this chapter from the practitioner's point of view.

Managing Risk: What School Did Not Teach Me

One way to approach risk is from the perspective of volatility: a stock declining in price or returns falling below one's expectations. Another school of thought comes from Warren Buffett and Benjamin Graham—it looks at risk as permanent loss of capital. Are these definitions mutually exclusive? The truth lies somewhere in between.

What risk means to us is shaped by our time horizon. If you are investing for the long run—at least five years—a permanent loss of capital is the risk that you should be concerned with the most. The distinction here is that if you are armed with a long-term time horizon, volatility is a mere inconvenience (and often an opportunity, especially in a sideways market). Assuming the volatility is temporary in nature, given enough time the investment will come back to its original level.

If you have a short-term time horizon, to you volatility is not temporary. Even a temporary stock decline results in permanent loss of capital, since you don't have the time to wait it out. Permanent loss of capital is a true risk to the long-term investor, since time will not heal that problem. This book is written for long-term investors, and thus we approach risk as permanent loss of capital.

There is another important, although less tangible, issue with volatility: It impacts our emotions and makes us do the wrong things—buy high and sell low. For a very rational computer-like decision maker this is not an issue. But we are not computers. Therefore, you shouldn't ignore the emotional element of volatility. Make reasonable attempts to minimize its impact on the portfolio through diversification, and/or own stocks whose businesses you understand, so that you can be comfortable with their price fluctuations.

Knowing the past is essential to being able to predict the future. But the past provides only one (though definitive) version of what could have taken place. Identify other possible pasts. "A winner is not to be judged" is a popular but dangerous Russian expression. This is a very common attitude when executive decisions, company performance or investment results are analyzed: Since it worked, it must have been a good decision.

~

All of life is management of risk, not its elimination.
—*Walter Wriston, former chairman of Citicorp*

Alternative History

Here is an example of how dangerous it is to evaluate decisions by focusing solely on the outcome. Let's say the CEO of a company that has all of its operations in Grand

Cayman decided to save a lot of money by canceling the company's hurricane insurance, saying something to his constituents along the lines of, "Why waste millions of dollars on insurance when we can put it into R&D instead?"

With God's help and a little bit of luck there was no hurricane the first year. The company saved a lot of money on insurance premiums, and its earnings went through the roof, marking the best year in its history. Now, should the CEO be given a huge bonus for saving millions of dollars on insurance premiums, or should he be fired?

Hindsight analysis based on observed history would tell us to reward the CEO. He did not waste money on insurance and saved millions of dollars.

But this conclusion completely ignores other very probable alternative paths and risk that has not surfaced—hidden risk. Analysis of what could have taken place, a look at alternative historical paths, would tell us the other, arguably more accurate side of the story. From 1871 to 2004, a hurricane hit Grand Cayman about every two-and-a-quarter years. In other words, there is a 44 percent possibility that a hurricane will hit Grand Cayman in any given year. This estimate is based on 133 years of historical observations, a pretty large data set.

If we gain an understanding of alternative historical paths then we will be able to assess the past more accurately—and thus gain a better understanding of the future.

In our example, the company's substantially improved profitability was accompanied (actually, generated!) by a very great hidden risk. The CEO had absolutely no control and no predictive forecasting power over if and when a hurricane would hit Grand Cayman. Unless he accurately predicted about a million different factors that impact the creation and direction of hurricanes, the CEO made a very blind decision that exposed the company to grave risk, and then just got lucky.

By analyzing results only in the context of observed risk, we subject ourselves to the mercy of randomness, because it determines how much risk to expose. When evaluation of results is based solely on observed risk, success is often attributed to skills of an investment or a corporate manager, and not to Lady Luck, who really deserves it.

In 2006 or early 2007, a broker who had his clients' accounts with my company called me and asked why our accounts were not doing as well as a mutual fund that he held in his personal account. I looked up that mutual fund and found that, though our accounts were up nicely for the year, the mutual fund was up double or triple what we were. I took a closer look and discovered that more than half of the fund's assets were in energy-related stocks, and this allocation was responsible for all of the fund's spectacular returns; at that time oil was making all-time highs. My response to the broker was simple: "Performance of this mutual fund will be driven in large part by a very volatile and unpredictable commodity—oil. You see the spectacular returns now, but what you don't see is the risk that has been taken by this fund. You don't have to have a rich imagination to picture what would happen to the returns of this fund if oil prices were to fall. I would never let this fund manager run my parents' money, or my kids' for that matter—the hidden risk [which showed up within a few years] is just too great."

Next time you hear a mutual fund or hedge fund manager bragging about the outsized returns of his fund with very little (observed) risk, remember our discussion about randomness and question alternative historical paths. Maybe it was all skill, but maybe the fund took a lot of risk through significant leverage or by placing very large bets on a single sector. Lady Luck may have been on his side up to this point but might not be in the future. Think about the cost of being wrong. What if Lady Luck had taken a day or a month off? What would have happened to the fund then?

This is why it is useful to analyze mutual funds or money managers looking at their worst-period results, not average longer-term returns; but even this may not reveal the embedded hidden risk. For instance, Amaranth, a large hedge fund, had phenomenal performance until . . . it did not. It placed large leveraged bets on the direction of the price of natural gas in the summer and fall of 2006. The fund did very well until it lost billions of dollars in less than a month. Such an event is the reason why, in your analysis of money managers or mutual funds, you want to make sure that their investment process makes sense to you. If it doesn't, even if past returns are terrific, stay away.

The investing environment is infested with randomness—it is a continual professional hazard. Our skill, knowledge, and experience should help to reduce the risk of randomness, but completely eradicating it is impossible, since randomness is the nature of the investing jungle. Stay within your circle of competence and do in-depth research to decrease the amount of randomness and its impact on your portfolio. Focus not only on what has happened (which is often random) but also on what could have happened. Learn from the past and judge companies and managers based on all possible outcomes. Finally, to help protect yourself from randomness—diversify!

Diversification: Not Always a Free Lunch

It is frequently said that diversification is the only free lunch an investor will ever get, since this risk-reduction strategy doesn't need to lead to a subsequent reduction in return. Or does it? Warren Buffett disagrees: "Diversification is a protection against ignorance. It makes little sense for those who know what they are doing."

Both statements are correct. At one extreme, investors often fail to diversify, holding just a handful of companies and subjecting themselves to unnecessary risk. The following happened to a good friend of mine. Let's call him Jack. He and his wife both worked for the largest insurance broker in the world, Marsh & McLennan, a much-respected firm with a market capitalization of over $20 billion and revenues in excess of $12 billion. Over the years, Jack and his wife accumulated a large position in Marsh's stock, which they were reluctant to sell.

Sometime in 2000 he asked me what I thought of their financial situation, having all this wealth in Marsh's stock. I commented that although I didn't see Marsh going out of business anytime soon, I would not recommend having all of their net worth in one company. Employees of Enron, MCI, or Lucent did not foresee their 401(k)s disappearing just months before they did so. Although the probability of Marsh disappearing was very, very small, this couple's lack of diversification was just not worth the risk, especially considering that both of their personal income streams (paychecks) also came from Marsh. Jack listened to my advice and agreed with it. He did not feel the urgency to do anything about it, though, stayed busy with his day-to-day life, and did not take action, until. . . .

Several years later, one sunny day (at least it was sunny on my side of Denver), I was driving to work when I got a call from Jack, who asked, "Did you see what happened to Marsh?" I had not. Jack explained that Eliot Spitzer (the state attorney general of New York at the time) had filed a lawsuit against Marsh accusing the company of bid rigging, insinuating that Marsh was not acting in clients' best interests when it charged (often undisclosed) contingent commissions. Marsh's stock was almost halved on the news, since contingent commissions accounted for a large portion of the company's profits. Talk about bankruptcy was in the air. To my surprise, Jack was very calm (considering that Marsh stock was his entire net worth at the time), and he asked my thoughts on what he and his wife should do about their Marsh stock.

In this type of situation, when all hell is breaking loose, you need to weigh the probabilities of possible outcomes. Bankruptcy, which was an improbable outcome for Marsh a day before the lawsuit was filed, suddenly became a lot more probable. Or at least the odds went from one in a gazillion to a remote but imaginable outcome. Marsh's debt did not seem high, at about 30 percent of total assets; however, without contingent commissions (whose future was very uncertain and which carried almost 100 percent gross margin), Marsh was barely profitable, if at all. Also, this had a similar smell to then recent Arthur Andersen debacle. Both firms were in the intellectual capital, or trust, business, in which a lawsuit could trigger a massive client exodus putting the company out of business.

If Marsh was just another stock (one of 15 or 20) in a diversified portfolio, the remote risk of its bankruptcy— the worst-case scenario—would have been considered as one of the risks, with appropriate attribution of probabilities to each potential outcome. But this is what theory doesn't tell you: When one cannot afford a low-probability outcome (and Jack could not afford it), one starts treating that outcome as having a much-increased probability.

Following our conversation, Jack sold a good portion of his Marsh stock at a significant loss. At the time the Marsh debacle was taking place, he was going to buy a new house, but he had to break the contract. He lost his down payment, plus he was not sure he and his wife would have their jobs down the road. Luckily, neither of them lost their jobs, and several months later he went to work for another insurance broker (the move was a promotion; working for Marsh was not the same anymore). I bet Jack will never look at diversification with the same complacency again.

Portfolio consisting of just a handful of stocks enormously impairs your ability to make rational decisions at the time when that ability is needed the most—under pressure. Managing this emotional reality is one of the more subjective aspects of risk management through diversification.

≈

I cannot be in 50 or 75 things. That's a Noah's Ark way of investing—you end up with a zoo that way. I like to put a meaningful amount of money into few things.

—Warren Buffett

Too Many Eggs, or Too Many Baskets?

At the other extreme, investors holding hundreds of stocks incur another cost—ignorance. The dictionary defines ignorance as the condition of being uneducated, unaware, or uninformed—the costs Buffett is referring to. A very large number of companies in investors' portfolios makes it impossible for them to know these companies well. Lack of knowledge leads to an inability to make rational decisions, which then causes investors to behave irrationally and hurts portfolio returns. Another side effect of over-diversification is indifference to individual investment decisions. In a portfolio of hundreds of stocks, an individual position might represent 1 percent or less of the total portfolio. The cost of being wrong is very small, as is the benefit of being right. If, for instance, one stock goes up or down 20 percent, the overall impact on the portfolio is only 0.20 percent either way. This breeds a semi-indifference to incremental decisions that is common among over-diversified buy-and-hold investors.

You need to strike an appropriate balance, weighing the consequences of either extreme. Academics disagree on the exact number of uncorrelated stocks needed in a portfolio to eradicate individual stock risk, but that number is usually given as somewhere between 16 and 25 stocks. This is another case where being vaguely right is better than being precisely wrong. I find that a portfolio of about 20 stocks is manageable and provides an adequate level of diversification; at this level, the price of being wrong is not too high, but every decision matters.

Taking diversification a step further, stress testing a portfolio (playing out different what-if scenarios) is critical, since it exposes weaknesses of the portfolio in the case of hidden risks rising to the surface.

Chapter Seventeen

I Could Be Wrong, but I Doubt It

~

MAYBE THE SIDEWAYS MARKET I'VE DESCRIBED is not in the cards. Maybe we are about to embark on the biggest bull market in U.S. history. We can study the conditions that preceded different markets, learn from them, and thereby form an educated forecast. Although conditions that preceded previous sideways markets are firmly in place and the probability of a sideways market unfolding over the next decade is high, it is clearly not certain.

Every strategy should be evaluated not just on a "benefit of being right" but, at least as importantly, on a "cost of being wrong" basis, and so let's do just that with Active Value Investing.

Look for your choices, pick the best one, then go with it.

—*Pat Riley*

In the unlikely case that a secular bull market will unfold in the near future (especially unlikely with stock valuations still at the level where the previous sideways market started), Active Value Investing will not punch the lights out, and no, it will not get you inducted into the hall of investing fame, but it should produce solid returns. After all, you own high-quality companies that are growing earnings, maybe even paying fat dividends, and you bought them at the right prices—with appropriate margin of safety.

Although we do have one-half of the components in place for a bear market to start—high valuations—chances are that, unless there is a tremendous long-term deterioration in the economy, a bear market will not show its sharp claws.

The only bear-market scenario under which Active Value Investing would produce results inferior to those of very high quality bond portfolio, is that of a prolonged recession coincident with or caused by deflation (similar to Japan's current bear market). Default-free Treasury bonds should do well in that type of environment; however, corporate bonds below those of top quality probably will not do well, since default rates would likely skyrocket.

In a bear market caused by or coinciding with high inflation and rising interest rates (Germany during World War I), bonds would deliver terrible real returns. In this case, the cost of being wrong while in bonds would be high, especially with long-term bonds, since their cash flows would be fixed for a long period of time, dramatically eroding your real purchasing power in the meantime.

Finally, the active buy-and-sell process should work to your advantage in a sideways market that is not going anywhere but has plenty of two-sided volatility. Cash being a residual of your investment decisions should only help you, providing much-needed dry powder to strike when future opportunities (stocks meeting all QVG criteria) present themselves. High-dividend-yielding stocks would be the source of an important portion of your portfolio's returns, as they have been in the previous sideways markets.

Active Value Investing is an even more attractive strategy if you consider the probabilities of each type of market occurring over the next decade. Looking at history as a guide, probability of the current sideways market staying with us for quite a while is high, but probability of a bear or, especially, a bull market taking hold is very low. Active Value Investing should be your strategy of choice!